# The Life and Times of Dave "The Rave" Stallworth

*A View from the Bench and the Stands*

Bob Powers #14 (1964-65 Final Four Teammate)

Robert Litan (Sports Enthusiast)

Copyright © 2022
All Rights Reserved

All royalties from the sale of this book will be donated to the WSU Foundation for the David Stallworth Memorial Scholarship

# Table of Contents

Acknowledgments ................................................................ i

Preface: Looking Back ........................................................ 1

Chapter One: Growing Up .................................................. 6

Chapter Two: The Path to Wichita ................................... 16

Chapter Three: Dave the Rave Arrives ............................ 33

Chapter Four: Dave and the Shockers Come Oh So Close 45

Chapter Five: Dave's Final "Half" Season ...................... 60

Chapter Six: Our Near Miracle ......................................... 67

Chapter Seven: Dave On and Off the Court .................... 85

Chapter Eight: The Ups and the Downs of the College Basketball Life ................................................................... 91

Chapter Nine: The Knicks and Dave's Too Brief NBA Career ................................................................................ 108

Chapter Ten: Life after Basketball ................................. 123

Chapter Eleven: Honoring Dave Forever ...................... 141

Epilogue ............................................................................ 177

About the Authors ........................................................... 184

A Final Note ..................................................................... 191

# Acknowledgments

We have written this book about the life of David Stallworth primarily for basketball fans of all ages in Wichita, Kansas, though we hope fans of other college teams also will be interested. Many who had the privilege to see Dave play, in person or on television, view him as the greatest athlete ever to wear a Wichita State Shocker uniform.

The numbers about his record – included at the back of the book – if anything, understate his impact. When Dave played, freshmen couldn't play varsity, so his numbers only cover three years of college play. Speaking of the number three, there was no three-point line back then. Dave's scoring average easily would have exceeded 30 points per game if there had been.

In this book, we tell the Dave Stallworth story both on and off the court. A story of a boy growing up on the wrong side of Dallas from a low-income family as a high school phenom who was overlooked by most major basketball programs, largely because he was black. His extraordinary college basketball career. His too-brief NBA career cut short by a heart ailment. And then, most of his adult life, as a father, husband, and quiet presence in Wichita, the city where his national stardom was born.

We write from two unique perspectives. Bob Powers writes not just as a former teammate but from the bench. Because, you see, that is where he sat during the one and a half years he was on the team with Dave. Powers watched his greatness from there and during practice. While both of us have written this book together, much of it is written in Bob Powers' "voice". We'll tell you where.

Robert Litan has co-authored this book from a (super) fan's perspective, dating from his childhood in Wichita. In reading this book, readers will understand what engaged Litan to undertake not only this project but also a prior one, with Powers, in chairing a committee to raise funds to erect a statue of Dave after his passing in 2017. That statue was dedicated in December 2018 and now greets fans as they enter Wichita State's home stadium, Koch Arena.

The two of us thoroughly enjoyed the research for and the writing of this book, blending what we learned and knew about Dave before undertaking this project with what we rediscovered from old newspaper articles and what other people whose lives Dave touched told us.

Bob Powers wants to thank his beautiful bride JoAnn; there aren't enough thanks he can give her. God gave Bob and JoAnn to each other. For fifty-five years, they have been at each other's side.

Bob also is grateful that he has been blessed to have eight wonderful children and twenty-four grandchildren. He loves them all equally. But he wants to highlight the authorial success of his son, Austin, who has struggled with severe Crohn's disease throughout his life. In the act of extraordinary courage, in addition to his everyday courage of living with the disease, Austin wrote a book about his difficult journey, *The Ostomy Guy Story: Memoirs of a Bagman*. Bob is so proud of Austin's amazing accomplishments, not only in telling his story but in raising his wonderful family and having a successful career despite his difficulties, which go way beyond Bob's. Although Bob Powers is now even with Austin in books written, he will never be even with Austin in the courage department.

Bob Litan wants to thank his wonderful wife Margaret for the privilege of being her husband and for her support for this project. Bob and Margaret first bonded over basketball, and for both of them, basketball has been central to their lives. Litan also dedicates this book to his two children, Ari and Alisa, their spouses, Amanda and Jake, and his grandchildren, Atticus Melanie, Yael and Liora, whom Bob hopes will be as enthusiastic about basketball as their grandfather.

# Preface: Looking Back

Neither of us was ever close friends of David Stallworth, one of the greatest basketball players ever to wear a Wichita State (and before that Wichita University) uniform.

Powers was his teammate, however, for one and a half years (readers will learn the reason for the 'half' in this book). He played against him in practice up close and personal every day during that charmed time in his life.

Powers saw that Dave could do things with a basketball that fans who saw him play could not believe. But unlike many sports superstars today, Dave was humble – not fake humble, but the real thing.

Powers also saw that Dave played basketball with the same kind, gentle, sharing way he lived his life. He never saw him lose his temper or yell at anyone. Gloria, his wife of thirty years, may take issue with that observation, but Powers never saw it happen. Not on the floor. Not on the street. Not anywhere with another human being.

Before beginning this project, neither of us knew much about Dave's early pre-Wichita years. Dave was quiet and reserved and didn't talk much about his growing up, not only when Powers played with him but when he would see him many years later. So, we both had to do some homework about his early years for this book.

We were fortunate that many people who knew Dave were willing to talk with us and shed light on parts of his life. We want to thank each one of them:

- Tony Morocco, Dave's close friend while he was at Wichita and a teammate on Dave's freshman team.

- Melvin Reed, a teammate of Dave's for years in Wichita. Mel was recruited to play from Ft. Worth, Texas, and played against Dave in high school.

- Lanny Van Eman, Dave's assistant coach for one and a half years, and his assistant coach for another year. Lanny is another former Shocker great who had a terrific coaching career in college and in the NBA. You'll learn a lot more about him in multiple places in the book.

- Wilber Williams, the starting point guard on Dave's high school state championship team, Madison High in Dallas. Wilbur talked freely about these years, and we are grateful he did.

We also greatly benefitted from a terrific profile of Dave's life published by Brad Townsend in the *Dallas Morning News,* published in 2004 but republished on September 22, 2017, six months after Dave died. We couldn't find a copy of it on the Internet, but a shorter version of the article, was published in the same newspaper on March 18, 2017, under a different byline, Kevin Sharrington, which is available at:

https://www.dallasnews.com/high-school-sports/2017/03/18/former-madison-high-and-nba-star-dave-stallworth-stayed-gracious-despite-being-ignored-by-his-hometown/

Much of Dave's early life material comes from the original Townsend article.

We benefitted immensely and quote extensively from Ralph Miller's book, *Ralph Miller: Spanning the Game*. Ralph coached Dave from the time he stepped on campus until the end of the 1963-64 season when Miller moved on to Iowa.

Back issues of the *Wichita Eagle* and the *Wichita Beacon* (before the Eagle bought it) also proved priceless for recovering details of the key Wichita games described in the book. The accounts of most of the Shocker games provided in the book come directly from these sources.

For much of the material about Dave's career with the New York Knicks, we drew on an excellent essay written in 1970 by sportswriter Jay Neugboren for *Sport* magazine and republished in a blog called "From Way Downtown". The legendary Wichita Eagle's sports columnist, Bob Lutz, also provided some great material about Dave's famous 5th game of the NBA finals in 1970 in this 2015 blog:

https://www.kansas.com/sports/spt-columns-blogs/lutz-blog/article9688598.html.

Various New York Daily News issues also fleshed out some key parts of Dave's NBA career with the Knicks.

Mike Kennedy, the radio and later T.V. voice of the Shockers, provided valuable information about Dave's team in two videos: one made at breakfast in Wichita on the 50th anniversary of the Shocker's reaching the Final Four, https://www.youtube.com/watch?v=LJaHl4hPeCU, and the other at a dinner organized that weekend, at https://www.youtube.com/watch?v=iSBzz65ltU8. We also benefitted from talking with Mike about this project, and we thank him for allowing us to include his observations in this book.

Throughout the book, we have woven in some recollections of Dave from other teammates and, in some cases, of those now gone. Bob Powers is grateful to all of them for their friendship from their college days through today. We also thank them for their contributions to this book.

Finally, we are grateful to Gloria Stallworth, who was kind enough to have multiple interviews with us and provided not only the story of her life, but the insights about their lives after Dave retired from basketball, all of which are contained in Chapter Ten.

As we discuss in the closing chapter, Wichita State University has established the David Stallworth Scholarship Fund, awarded annually to an outstanding undergraduate majoring in education. We thank all those who have already contributed to this fund. All royalties from this book's sale will also be donated to the fund.

We dedicate this book to all those who have or will in the future support the David Stallworth Scholarship Fund, Gloria Stallworth, and the five children both Dave and Gloria raised. We wish them all much success and happiness in the future.

# Chapter One: Growing Up

David Stallworth came into this world, in Dallas, in 1941 — a year that will never be forgotten. The year our nation was attacked, triggering the entry of the United States into World War II.

We have written this book because we want to help ensure that Dave Stallworth also is never forgotten. He played a big role in Powers' life in college. Litan became a huge fan in his middle school years, and as you will learn, that love for Stallworth at a distance led to the close friendship between the two authors developed many years later. And to the projects we have both undertaken, including the writing of this book, to memorialize Stallworth, his life, and his legacy.

Dave Stallworth put Wichita, Kansas, the hometown of Wichita University, later Wichita State University, on the college basketball map. He made Wichita famous for more than just once being known as the "Air Capitol of the World".

In fact, Powers had never heard of Wichita until he was recruited to play basketball for the school. If not for basketball, he probably wouldn't have paid more than several seconds of attention to the city — unless it was on the national news for something or other — the rest of his life. Yet as fate would have it, after graduating from Wichita, the city has been Powers' home for nearly six decades.

Litan left Wichita after graduating high school but returned for several years in his 60s, largely to be able to watch the Wichita State basketball team in person as a season ticket holder. It was during this period that he met and bonded with Powers. Stallworth was the reason, as readers will learn.

Although Dave never went to the Final Four, he helped inspire an understaffed "Wheatshocker" team – Shockers, for short — he had to leave in the middle of his senior year when he graduated to get there. Against all odds, the Shockers made it to the Final Four the year Dave left. Powers was lucky to just be along for the ride as a teammate. Litan as a fan.

As much as we admire Dave, this isn't just another "hero worship: sportsbook". Of course, there was much about Dave that *was* heroic, sometimes superhuman. But Dave faced obstacles in his life, from the very beginning, all the way until the end. What is remarkable is not just his athletic talent — which was rare, to be sure — but how he dealt with life's setbacks. The peace and grace that characterized how Dave lived his life had a genetic component. But Dave was fortunate to have had a nurturing mother and coaches, as well as his loving wife of three decades, Gloria, whom you will meet later in this book.

So, as unique as Dave's talents were, the way he lived is what, to us, made him truly heroic. That's why we believe his story of enjoying some big ups and overcoming some big downs has such strong universal appeal.

\*\*\*

Dave had it hard from the start. He was born to and raised by a single mother on the south side of Dallas, the poor, tough part of an otherwise wealthy city. His mother worked hard as a maid at a Dallas hotel and later in a cafeteria. Dave's father had moved away to Los Angeles before he was born. Dave never knew him growing up.

Their neighborhood was called The Bottom. Asked by Brad Townsend, a reporter from the *Dallas Morning News* in 2004, about the reason why, Dave told like it was, as he always did: "Because that's what it was. The bottom of the totem pole."

Dave went on: "We were all dirt poor down there, but everybody knew each other, cared about each other, helped each other." Only someone with Dave's peaceful and forgiving temperament could say that even so, "I don't think

I would have enjoyed growing up in any place other than Dallas."

Townsend reports that Dave learned to play basketball at a local outdoor court because his elementary school didn't have a gym. He grew up idolizing two older high school stars at the time: Abner Haynes, the speedster receiver who starred for the American Football League's Dallas Texans, and Stone Johnson, who would later run sprints for the 1960 U.S. Olympic team and then played football for the Kansas City Chiefs. Tragically, Johnson died from a broken neck suffered in a preseason game in 1963 against the Houston Oilers in, of all places... Wichita, Kansas. The city where Dave would make his mark on the national stage.

\*\*\*

But first, he had to get in the game, so to speak. He did that one day in 9th grade by knocking on a closed gym door at Madison High School, asking to try out for the basketball team that was then in practice (Townsend reports it as 8th grade, but it must be a typo since high school doesn't start until 9th grade). Madison was a formerly all-white school, reopened to relieve overcrowding at two other predominantly black high schools, Lincoln and Washington.

Madison's first-year coach was Euril Henson, then a 28-year-old former basketball standout at Houston's Yates High

School and Prairie View A&M in college. It couldn't have been a hard decision to take Dave onto the team. At well over 6 feet at age 14, Dave was already one of the tallest kids.

Still, coaches do matter. And Henson was a great coach. Dave recalled to Townsend that Henson "taught me more about basketball than anybody I ran into in my whole life, period." That's a remarkable statement, given the many outstanding coaches, he would later play for.

It's also remarkable because, according to Dave's close friend and point guard on Madison's team, Wilbur Williams, Henson was a strict disciplinarian. And toughest of all on Dave, most likely because Henson knew he had such great talent.

Henson was also a stickler for neatness and professionalism. Everyone on the team had to wear coats and ties on game and travel days. No exceptions, no excuses.

Henson coached his team as a *team*. No one, not even Dave, and indeed especially Dave, got special treatment. Even to the point of holding down Dave's scoring — benching him if he came close to scoring 20 points — to ensure that everyone on the team could contribute. We hear a lot today about hitting the "Open Man", one of the hallmarks of how the Golden State Warriors play. Well, Henson was ahead of his time, constantly telling his players he didn't care how open they were. If someone else was even more open, players had to pass it to him.

Henson drilled into his players the same team mentality on defense. If a teammate was having problems covering his man, then others on the team had better be ready to help.

These team rules were strictly enforced. Violate them, and Henson would bench a player.

With Henson's guidance and help from his teammates, Stallworth put Madison on Texas' basketball map. Historically, high school teams from Houston dominated the state tournament. Dave changed that, though it took a bit of time.

Playing center at 6' 5" — he would later grow another two inches in college — Dave and his Madison teammates didn't get past the first round of the state tournament in his sophomore year. Madison went a bit further in the state tournament the following year, beating Booker T. Washington out of Houston along the way. Williams recalled to Powers that game being "One of the greatest games that he had even been part of," with Madison coming out on top 88-84. That junior year Dave was all-state.

In Dave's senior year, Madison really arrived, making it to the final round of the state championship in 1960, where Madison faced another Houston team, Kashmere Gardens.

Unbelievably, the title game never was played. The arena was so crowded with fans from Dallas and Houston — after all, this was an unusual showdown — and the fans apparently were so rowdy that they crowded the floor *before* the game and wouldn't leave. It was a Saturday night. Williams recalls that the officials running the tournament told everyone in the crowd that the game had to be postponed. The Madison team thought the game would be rescheduled for the next day, Sunday, and crowds had returned. As game time approached, state officials apparently believed the game could not be played safely, so they simply declared both teams co-champs. Williams, who still lives in Texas, believes this was the first, and still is, the only time in Texas that co-champs were declared without the high school finals being played.

Dave again was all-state his senior year. But a little-known fact about Dave is that basketball was not his only sport. Williams recalls Dave being an outstanding receiver in football (where his high school nickname was "Long") and first basemen in baseball (being a good hitter and fielder). In Chapter Seven, you will learn some more incredible facts about Dave's athletic talents.

Being active in multiple sports had to help Dave in each one of them. But basketball was special for Dave, where his dedication to all aspects of the game no doubt helped make him a superstar.

One story about his work ethic stands out. Today in the NBA, big men have mastered all facets of the game. Think of Nikola (the "Joker") Nokic, Joel Embid, Anthony Davis, Kevin Durant, and Giannis Atentokounmpo, among others. Each of them is not only great in the "post" but also on the perimeter. They play like huge point guards.

Although Dave never grew to 7' range, he wasn't satisfied with the typical post-play of being a center in high school. High school teammate Williams recalls that Dave would find a coach and practice dribbling and passing after every practice. Those skills later would help make him into a college superstar as a forward. Indeed, as his college career was nearing its end, Dave told a reporter for the *Wichita Beacon* (the city's afternoon paper that eventually was bought by the *Eagle*) why he passed so often, despite being the dominant scorer on the team: "Why should I take a 60 percent shot when I can pass to a man within 90 percent range? The team is out to win, and this is the best way I know how to help."

Readers can see the influence of Coach Henson in that statement. In Williams' words, "Dave never tells himself that he was a star." The team-first attitude instilled by

Henson into all his players, including Dave, didn't change as Dave moved up the basketball ranks. As one of his college teammates, Jon Criss, stated, "Dave was a great team player, never complained, never acted like the game was about him."

And hard as it is to believe, Williams says at "James Madison he didn't stand out." He was just part of his team, part of the "franchise". Dave would soon be much more than that in his next four years.

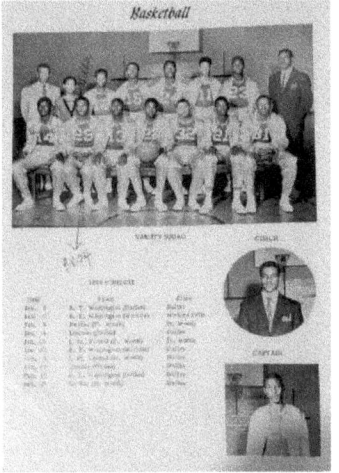

James Madison High School (1959-1960)

Dave and his teammates

Basketball and Golf

## Chapter Two: The Path to Wichita

Here's more that's hard to believe. As good as he was in high school – all-state two years in a row – Dave was recruited by only one school, other than Wichita, outside of Texas. With all his talent and renown throughout Texas, you might ask, how could that be? The answer, unfortunately, is all too simple: he was black.

At the time Dave graduated high school in the middle of the 1960-61 school year, few black basketball players from Texas were recruited by out-of-state colleges (Wichita, as you will learn later in this chapter, was one of them). The black players capable of playing ball at the college level just expected it would be for a historically black school inside the state, like Prairie View or Texas Southern.

To be sure, Dave had dreamed of attending one Texas school that was not a historically black college – Southern Methodist (SMU), which had a great sports tradition at that time. Many years later, SMU was severely punished by the NCAA for under-the-table payments made to its football players, a practice we're pretty sure was widespread at the time. SMU just got caught. In any event, attending SMU was out of the question for Dave. He was black, and SMU hadn't yet started recruiting black players for any sports.

So how did Dave Stallworth, who became a Wichita basketball icon, end up in *Wichita, Kansas?*

Two people know the answer to that question, they both knew each other well, yet they have somewhat different accounts.

Those individuals are the late Ralph Miller, Dave's coach for all but his last semester at Wichita, and Lanny Van Eman, the great Shocker shooting guard who played from 1959 through 1962. Lanny coached Dave as Ralph's assistant after Lanny graduated. Lanny also recruited Powers to play basketball at Wichita, as you will learn in Chapter Four.

Ralph and Lanny are so important to the Stallworth era that readers first deserve to know a bit about their own backgrounds before we relate how each claims Stallworth was persuaded to become a Shocker.

***

Ralph Miller grew up in a small town about 100 miles east of Wichita, Chanute. At his local high school in the late 1930s, he starred in football, as a quarterback, and basketball. When we say "starred", we really mean starred. He was so good he was recruited to play both sports by Kansas, where the legendary "Phog" Allen (or Dr. Allen, as most called him) was coaching basketball, and by Stanford.

Indeed, according to his autobiography, *Spanning the Game,* Miller was all set to go to Stanford after a campus visit but changed his mind at the last minute to attend K.U.

Miller had an outstanding career in both sports at K.U., and although suffering a knee injury midway through his time there, he had some big games. K.U.'s basketball team on which he played advanced pretty far several times in the NCAA's fledgling national tournament. Most important for his future career, Miller was instructed by then the most innovative college basketball coach in the country, Dr. Allen. Miller would absorb lessons from Allen that he would improve upon later when Miller himself coached.

Coaching came right away after Miller's graduation, in the middle of World War II. As he tells it in *Spanning the Game*, after he joined the Air Force, a corporal found out about Miller's sports excellence and his degree in physical education. That corporal told his commanding officer about Miller, and shortly thereafter, Miller's desire to be a physical instructor was fulfilled. That instructorship assignment, which he retained at several bases inside the forty-eight states over three years, kept Miller away from the fronts in the war and may have saved his life.

After the war, Miller bounced around a few jobs before he was asked to bethe basketball coach at Wichita's East

High School in the late 1940s. His immediate success, culminating in the state championship in 1951, came to the attention of Wichita University President Harry Corbin, a basketball fan himself. Corbin had little trouble convincing Miller to become the Shockers' coach that same year.

Miller brought with him to Wichita the star on Wichita East's high school team, Cleo Littleton, who went on to become one of Wichita's great players as an undersized forward at 6' 3". Cleo's size didn't stop him from scoring an average of nearly 20 points per game during his four-year career – first-year students were allowed in those days to play varsity. He remains the Shocker's all-time scoring leader, with 2164 points, and was named an all-American his senior year.

The Shockers' fortunes continued to improve through the mid-1950s under Miller's guidance, enough to encourage the university to build a state-of-the-art basketball arena. Henry Levitt Arena, or the Roundhouse as it soon came to be called, opened in 1955. With a little more than 10,000 seats, more than double the size of the old Wichita Forum where the Shockers formerly played, the Roundhouse was a state-of-the-facility that other colleges later copied throughout the country.

Miller reports in his book that many were skeptical that his teams could fill the arena, which contributed to the reluctance of university officials at the time to spend an additional $125,000 – on top of the $1.5 million original cost — to raise the roof by another 25 feet, which would have accommodated another 7,000-8,000 fans. By the time Stallworth and his teammates arrived in the 1960s, tickets to Shocker games became the biggest thing in town, and there would have been no trouble filling the place up.

Miller was a tough disciplinarian. Jon Criss, one of Dave's teammates and Powers, pretty much summed it up at the 50th anniversary of the 1965 team's Final Four appearance when he reminded the audience that Miller was called by his players "Ralph the Ripper" for a reason. Lanny confirms that name in a quotation in Miller's own autobiography! Miller's players also called him another nickname behind his back, "Alligator Hide", referring to his rough exterior. That name doesn't appear in Miller's book.

Miller's temper and toughness did not prevent many players from respecting him. At that same 50th anniversary breakfast, Stallworth was asked to compare Miller with his New York Knicks coach, the legendary Red Holzman. Stallworth replied that while Holzman coached the team,

Miller was the one who coached *him* and said it with admiration and respect.

In his autobiography, Miller was proud of his record in recruiting and coaching black athletes, which was unheard of at the time. Nonetheless, as a freshman participating with the varsity in practice, he seemed to be unusually tough toward black players. I prefer to believe it was because he expected more of them, which was his way of pushing them. Or maybe Miller's interpersonal skills just didn't match his basketball genius.

And it was genius. For example, Miller was way ahead of his time in constantly having his teams press and run. Miller's teams had to be in super shape to pull this off, but that pressure wore opponents down. In games decided by 2 or 3 points, that could make all the difference.

Miller was especially famous for his 2-2-1 zone press defense, which his teams played after made baskets, even free throws. The 2-2-1 meant that two defensive players would guard the in-bounds play, two at roughly midcourt, with a center hanging back. Miller used and refined that defense, which UCLA's legendary John Wooden adopted and perfected with a decade of superior athletes in the 1960s and 1970s.

Miller introduced another innovation. Since basketball was a fast game, he didn't want players thinking too much but instead automatically reacting. Practices developed team muscle memory, so every player knew where he had to be and where to find others. In the same spirit, to cut down on confusion about who his players had to guard on defense, Miller had a simple rule: guard the man who guarded you.

And he tended to the little things, like teaching his players to keep their hands down and low while on defense. The harder to make it for officials to call fouls.

Miller coached Wichita through the 1963-64 season but left the Shockers before the magical 1964-65 season when the team took an improbable ride to the Final Four. Many Shockers, including me (Powers), were sorry to see him go. After all, he had recruited the entire team, and the fear of the unknown – whether we would get less playing time under a new, different coach – loomed larger than whatever fears the players had about him in practice every day. After going to Iowa, Miller went to Oregon State, finishing his college coaching career in 1989. He notched over 300 wins, a 63 percent winning rate, and had only three losing seasons.

***

Unlike Miller's tough guy persona, Lanny was more like Gary Thompson, who played for Miller in the 1950s, later served as his assistant, and then replaced him after Miller departed for Iowa.

In other words, Lanny was a players' coach. The difference between Miller and Lanny probably had something to do with the fact that the two grew up in different generations.

Lanny was one of the great Shocker shooting guards, averaging 14 points per game over his three-and-a-half-year career at Wichita. The half was because Lanny started out at North Carolina State, was deeply unhappy, and over a remarkable weekend in January 1958, transferred and began playing for Wichita.

As Lanny recounts in Miller's book: "I think I took my final exam at N.C. State on maybe Thursday, and hitchhiked home on Friday. My brother met me out on the Pennsylvania turnpike… Saturday night, I went to the Duke-West Virginia game. Both of them had recruited me. When I got home, I called Ralph. He said, 'Can you get an airplane out tomorrow?' I flew to Wichita on Monday and was going to class on Tuesday."

Lanny grew up in McKeesport, Pennsylvania, a small town outside of Pittsburgh. He came to Wichita because he knew about the pipeline of basketball players from the

McKeesport area that Wichita's sports programs had already established.

That pipeline began with the Shocker's football coach in the early 1950s, Pittsburgh native Jim Trimble, who recruited football players from McKeesport. Before coming to Wichita, Trimble recruited NFL legend Johnny Unitas, for a semi-pro team. In Miller's first year, two Wichita football players from McKeesport, George, and Sneak Thomas, told Miller about a basketball star from the area, Jim McNerney. Although Miller was skeptical, he invited McNerney out and was soon convinced he could play college ball at a high level. McNerney was Wichita's first of many McKeesport recruits.

In the (very) small world department, McNerney would later coach the Wichita Southeast High School basketball team in the 1960s. In McNerney's last year, one book's co-authors, Bob Litan, worked for him as the team's basketball manager. Litan would later do the same for two years under Dave Leach, Powers' teammate in Wichita for two years.

Back to McKeesport. In recruiting McNerney, Miller reports in his autobiography that he struck up a friendship with the high school basketball coach, Neenie Campbell (how's that for a first name?). Soon, Miller says his recruiting consisted largely of simply calling up Neenie and asking who should come to Wichita next. It gives you an idea of how much – or actually, how little – Miller cared about recruiting, a job he would later delegate to his assistant coaches throughout his career. The recruiting of Stallworth, which we will soon address, was not much more intensive than Miller's McKeesport recruiting.

Eventually, over twenty-three McKeesport exports would come to Wichita, including two of the Wichita greats, forward Ron Heller and Van Eman. Both would become Wichita assistant coaches.

As we recount in a later chapter, Lanny was not just a great shooter, especially in the clutch, but also an excellent shortstop in baseball. So good that he played both sports at Wichita. After graduation, he played briefly for the New York Yankee's minor league farm team before returning to Wichita to begin as an assistant coach for Miller in the 1962-63 season (though he turned down an offer to join the Milwaukee Braves' major league team, a difficult decision he told us, but one he made because he didn't want to burn his bridges with Miller). Lanny recruited Powers the following year.

Lanny followed Miller to Iowa and Oregon State before getting his first head coaching job at Arkansas, where one of his teams won the (then) Southwest Conference. Lanny later graduated to the NBA, where he had assistant jobs with the Boston Celtics (during the Larry Bird era) and the Dallas Mavericks.

***

So, then, how did Dave Stallworth end up in Wichita? Today, coaches from throughout the country would have been crawling all over him with his talent. Not in those years for reasons already stated.

Here's Miller's story about he found Stallworth, based on Miller's autobiography, a story which seems to be the conventional wisdom.

Even while Stallworth was in high school and no one outside Texas had heard of him, Miller had already established a Texas pipeline of players headed to Wichita in the late 1950s who played for the Shockers through the early 1960s.

First, there was Jonny Gales, a 6' 5" forward from Ft. Worth. Miller doesn't indicate how he heard of Gales but recounted that he took a gamble on him – which proved successful – because it was hard then for out-of-Texas colleges to know much about Texas high school basketball players. Of course, Miller could have *gone down* to Texas to look for himself, but as we noted earlier, recruiting and Miller didn't mix well.

Next, Linwood Sexton, an All-American football player at Wichita, put Miller in touch with a relative in Amarillo, Texas, 6' 10" Gene Wiley. Miller worked hard to get Wiley, who had dropped out of high school but had artistic talent (and later in life he *became* an artist after finishing his basketball career). Miller arranged a job for Wiley in Wichita that helped pay his expenses while he finished high school at Wichita East. After graduation, Miller had him enrolled at Wichita. Wiley had superior defensive and rebounding skills – enough to later become a second-round draft choice of the Los Angeles Lakers – but rarely shot, though when he did, he shot well. Miller regretted not teaching him more about shooting and other offensive skills. If he had done so, Wiley would have scored much more than his Shocker career average of 10.6 points per game.

With Gales and Wiley, the Texas pump was primed, as it were. And ready for fate to intervene. Miller recounted that he had a friend, Rusty, who worked at Boeing and loved basketball and had been trying to send Miller more Texas high school recruits for some time. In 1960, according to Miller's account, Rusty was on a plane from Boston to Dallas. Several Olympic athletes, including Stone Johnson, were on the same flight, returning home after the Rome Olympics. Yes, the same Stone Johnson mentioned in

Chapter One, who had run fifth in the 200 meters at the 1960 Olympic Games, and who later tragically died in a pro football game in Wichita.

In talking with the Olympians on the plane, Miller reported that Rusty got around to talking with them about basketball, prompting Johnson to volunteer that the best high school basketball player in Texas was none other than Dave.

Rusty reported this to Miller, who asked Rusty to go down and "take a look". If Johnson were right about Dave, Miller would send his brother Dick, an assistant working with him, to see for himself. Again, Miller wouldn't go, only an assistant.

Rusty did as he was told and returned with this: "Ralph, he is the best basketball player I have ever seen in high school." Dick then went down and pretty much said the same: "Ralph, you've never had anybody as good as he is."

Although Oklahoma State came in at the last minute with an offer, Miller had Stallworth wrapped up by then.

The "Rusty" in Miller's telling was Rusty Taylor. Tommy Newman, later to come to Wichita in 1963, told us that Rusty had something to do with recruiting every player from Texas who played for Miller at Wichita.

To give you an idea of how humble Dave was, many years later, when interviewed by Townsend of the *Dallas Morning News*, Dave said (surely with a straight face): "As far as me being the best athlete to come of there [Dallas or Texas], I doubt it. I was a good athlete, but there were so many others who were outstanding."

Lanny has a slightly different recollection. He knew about Rusty, reporting that Rusty closely followed high school teams around the country by reading newspapers. Only when Rusty uncovered Stallworth through the local Dallas media, such as it was, did he then suggest to Miller that Stallworth be recruited. The rest of Lanny's story squares with Miller's.

Lanny also reports something that's not in Miller's book. Dave was sold on Wichita, as opposed to any other school, in or out of Texas, because he knew about the basketball strength of the Missouri Valley Conference and that black players played important roles on MVC teams. Not just at Wichita but also at Bradley, and especially at Cincinnati. Remember, this was when Oscar Robertson was the best player in college basketball, and the MVC was riding high as one of the best, if not *the* best, basketball conferences in the country.

The Big "O" would lead Cincy to the Final Four in both 1959 and 1960, years when Dave was tearing up the high school basketball circuit in Texas. Robertson left for the pros after the 1960 tournament, making history as a legendary NBA star and as the NBA player who brought free agency to that league (more about that in Chapter Ten).

Cincy would win the NCAA championship the next two years in a row (1961 and 1962) under a new coach, Ed Jucker, and miss out on a three-peat in 1963, when it lost to Loyola, Chicago, in an overtime game that is an NCAA championship classic. Loyola was lucky to win that game since Cincy unwisely went into a stall near the end of the game, blew its lead, and ended up in overtime that should never have been played. As you will learn in chapter 4, Wichita – with Stallworth by then – beat both of those NCAA title game teams that year.

Back to Dave's recruitment. Maybe both the Miller and Van Eman stories are true. Maybe Rusty already knew about Stallworth before he got on that plane, or maybe he read about him after returning from Boston. It doesn't matter. Somehow it was Rusty Taylor who was most responsible for Stallworth being recruited to play for Wichita.

Dave started at Wichita, as a freshman in the second semester of the 1960-61 season, right after graduating high school mid-year. That Miller played him as a freshman right away so he could have Dave join varsity mid-year the following year, during the 1961-62 season, was a fateful decision long-time Wichita fans remember to this day. Readers who don't already know the reason why will learn about it in the next chapter. And why it is one of those decisions that Miller also most regretted.

There is an exclamation point to add to the story of Dave's recruitment to Wichita, which also was an accident of fate. When Dick Miller went to Texas to see Stallworth play in a game that game turned out to be one pitting James Madison against a team from Ft. Worth. The center on that latter team was 6' 10" Nate Bowman, whom Dick Miller described as someone like Gene Wiley, who was already playing for Wichita but also without much basketball training. That didn't matter to Miller, most likely because of his positive experience with molding Wiley's raw talent. So, Miller called Bowman – again, he didn't visit – and asked Nate if he knew Stallworth, which Nate confirmed. Miller then asked if he, Bowman, would like to play alongside Stallworth in Wichita. It was an easy sell. Bowman immediately said yes.

Both Miller and Van Eman recall that Bowman's family – all twenty-four of them – came to see Wichita play North

Texas State later that spring to meet Miller in person. Bowman arrived on the Wichita campus, as a freshman, for the full 1961-62 basketball season. Together, he and Dave would make Wichita basketball history.

# Chapter Three: Dave the Rave Arrives

Dave Stallworth arrived on Wichita's campus for the first time in the winter of 1961 with just this: some tennis shoes slung over his shoulder and a bag of clothes. Coach Miller began walking him around campus, but Dave hung back two steps. Miller, as he recounted in his autobiography, asked Dave why. Stallworth answered, "Well, Coach, I'm from Texas, and in Texas, you walk two places behind a white man." Miller answered, "You're not in Texas now. You're in Wichita, and don't you ever forget it."

Stallworth started at Wichita in mid-year, right after graduating mid-year. Many Shocker fans may want to know why mid-year high school graduation. Well, here's the answer. Many years after he had retired from basketball, Dave told the long-time radio (and often TV) voice of the Shockers, Mike Kennedy, on one of Kennedy's broadcasts that he (Dave) was badly burned by boiling water in his younger years in the Dallas cafeteria where his mother was working. So badly burned that Dave had to stay out of school for some time. When he did come back later, he was back on a new schedule but graduated a semester *early* on that schedule. Hence, his early arrival in Wichita.

Dave was hyped from the very beginning. A February 1, 1961 article in the *Wichita Eagle* dubbed him "One of the most polished freshmen in WU history." He was then 6' 6", an inch shorter than the 6' 7" he would play at the following season and for the rest of his career. The *Eagle* reported that even at his first workout, he "looked ready… to play for the Shocker varsity right now."

His freshman play clearly validated that statement. Stallworth put up a freshman scoring record of 28 points per game. In one game, against Fort Hays, he hit 52 – demonstrating that if he wanted and the team required it, he could put up big numbers in any game. He would prove that time and again when he moved up to the varsity.

Miller could have kept Dave playing on the freshman team for the remainder of that 1961-62 season. But as we wrote in the last chapter, in a decision he later regretted, Miller was anxious to have Dave join the varsity as soon as it was legally possible. Miller wanted to do far more than just improve the team's 18-8 overall record and 5$^{th}$ place finish in the MVC conference the previous year. With Lanny graduating in January 1962, the Shocker's only real chance to win the MVC title that year would have to come from beginning to play Dave in the second half of that season. Dave would join a team with a young, outstanding backcourt

– sophomores Ernie Moore and Leonard Kelly – along with standout defensive center Gene Wiley.

Even so, it was a big gamble because Cincinnati was the heavy favorite to win the conference, having already won it and the national championship the previous year. In addition, while Wichita was 14-5 overall, its MVC record was just 4-3 before Dave joined the team. And as good as Dave had shown himself to be on the freshman team, Miller did know not know how dominant Stallworth would become once he joined the varsity.

Although Dave's play was outstanding, Miller lost the gamble, exceeding Miller's expectations. In Dave's first varsity game in 1962 against Marquette, in which the Shockers came from behind to win 79-71, Stallworth scored 18 points, right behind guard Ernie Moore's 24. Dave went on from there to become the team's leading scorer, averaging 20 points per game his first half season. But in the 7 remaining games of that first semester of Stallworth's eligibility, the team again went 4-3. Getting blown out by St. Louis and Cincinnati certainly didn't help. The Shocks finished up again at 18-8, though with a 3rd place ranking in the MVC with a 7-5 conference record.

Still, the Shocker's overall record was good enough to get the team into the post-season NIT, which was a much bigger deal than it is today. But the Shockers lost in the first round against a taller Dayton team, 79-71, despite overcoming an 11-point halftime deficit and at one point trailing by just two in the second half. Stallworth led the comeback and ended the game with a Shockers' game high of 18. But it wasn't enough, and the NIT loss ended their season.

Meanwhile, Cincinnati won the Valley title again and the national championship for the second year in a row.

*\*\**

The Shockers opened the 1962-63 season with much higher hopes. Wichita's sports information director had given Stallworth the nickname by which Wichita fans would already call him, "Dave the Rave". And Dave had more than just a "supporting cast". Not only was the Moore/Kelly backcourt returning, but Nate Bowman was coming out as a sophomore to take over the center duties from Wiley, who was off to the Lakers after the previous season. Senior Wayne Durham, a 6' 7" forward, was coming back, capable of hitting double figures on any given night. And the Shockers had a sharpshooting 6' 5" sophomore, Dave Leach, joining the varsity.

The Shocks were poised to become a national force in 1962-63, which in fact, they turned out to be. The team hovered in the top 10 in the Associated Press poll for much of the year, especially the latter half, and finished the regular season ranked 5th, with a 19-7 regular season record, earning second place in the Valley.

With that kind of record today, Wichita easily would have earned an at-large NCAA bid. But in those days, a team had to win the conference title to get into the NCAA tournament. Cincy again won that top spot, going all the way to the national title game for the 3rd year in a row.

Again, Wichita was invited to the NIT. And again, the team struck out, upset by one point in the first round by Villanova (a school that would emerge in the 1980s as one of the nation's premier college basketball programs, upsetting heavily favored Georgetown in the 1985 title game, with perhaps one of the greatest halves of shooting in NCAA tournament history).

While the Shocker team again did not advance as far in the post-season as many expected, Stallworth had emerged as the team's star in the 1962-63 season. His 22.6 points per game and 10.2 rebounds per game were, by far, the highest on the team.

Those two stats didn't do justice to Dave's game. One thing that every one of his teammates has repeated, in print or to us, is how unselfish Dave was. In writing about Dave more than 50 years later, *Wichita Eagle* columnist Bob Lutz recounts a recollection from Dave that one of the games he remembered most was one in which he only scored eight points but otherwise played well in all other facets of the game.

Dave could gently rib his teammates from time to time. Larry Nosich remembers a Shocker win against Arizona State on December 17, 1962. With four seconds to go and the game tied, Ralph Miller drew up a play for Dave Leach to take the ball and get it to Dave Stallworth. But because Stallworth was triple covered, Nosich remembers, Leach threw the ball to Larry at the top of the key. Knowing his driving skills weren't the greatest, Nosich shot the ball instead. And it went in!

Larry's heroics were the story's lead in the *Wichita Eagle* the next day. Nosich fondly recalled to us that Stallworth would rub it in that Nosich got more ink out of his shot than Dave did about the 38 points he scored. He did the *same thing* when the 1964-65 Shockers convened for a weekend in 2015 for their 50$^{th}$-anniversary reunion.

But it was all in good fun. Nosich says that Stallworth was one of the nicest guys he has ever known and that "you would never know being around him that he was a first-team All-American."

***

Mike Kennedy identifies two things about great players. One is that they take their God-given talents to the highest level by practice, practice, practice. The great ones are always in the gym, not just because they want to be great, but because they just *love* playing basketball. Michael Jordan, Kobe, LeBron, and, yes, Dave Stallworth. He just loved being in the gym because he just loved the game.

One of his teammates, Jon Criss, summed it up this way: "Dave was a basketball player's player. He had the size, speed and skill to become a two-time all-American. To me, his greatest attribute was his work ethic. He did everything full speed, 100%, all out, whether it was a basic drill in practice or grabbing a rebound and leading the fast break. Dave was all in — 100%."

The second characteristic of the great ones is that they are "clutch" – they come through in the big moments—the buzzer-beating shots. Taking over the game, sometimes even entire games, when they know their team requires it to win. Although Dave worked hard to get his entire team into each game, he would "turn it on" to score himself if he felt he needed to.

The highlight of the 1962-63 Shocker season came on February 16, 1963, because "turn it on" is precisely what

Dave did. Against then top-ranked Cincinnati, with a 37-game winning streak coming into the game played at the Roundhouse. Cincy also came into the game with the nation's best defense, holding opposing teams to less than 52 points per game. Led by its two under-sized forwards (by today's standards), 6' 5" junior Ron Bonham and 6" 2" senior Tom Thacker, who would later be named First-Team Consensus All-Americans. Six weeks earlier, Cincy had easily handled the Shockers on Cincy's home court, 63-50.

To be sure, the Shockers were no slouches coming into the February rematch. Earlier in the season, they had beaten both Purdue and Ohio State at the Roundhouse. And for several weeks in a row, the Shockers had been nationally ranked in the AP poll, though they had fallen out of the top ten right before the Cincy game because of a loss to St Louis on its home court.

Still, what happened that night was one of the greatest – if not the greatest – Shocker basketball games and victories of all time (the closest to it, in our minds, was the Shocker's upset of then number one ranked Gonzaga in the second round of the 2013 NCAA tournament, with two freshmen by the names of Ron Baker and Fred Van Vleet, both of whom would become All Americans). The game see-sawed, but one thing stood out: Cincy could not stop Dave Stallworth, who was hitting shots from all over the floor and then making his free throws after frequently being fouled.

Nonetheless, Cincy slowly built a small lead in the second half and was up by six with 3:30, despite Dave's 39 points. It looked hopeless for the Shockers, Cincy's defense looked tough, and this was before the three-point shot and the shot clock, both of which allow teams that many points behind to turn things around quickly.

Ralph Miller wasn't bothered, at least on the outside. Calmly and rather unbelievably, he reportedly told his team during a time-out huddle near the end of the game something to the effect, "Don't worry, Play your game. 'We've got them where we want them?' Huh?"

Well, it worked. As we have said, Dave would turn it on if he had to, and he then went out and topped the already remarkable performance he had put on to that point. In those last three-plus minutes, he scored 7 more, bringing his game total to 46, while Cincy's offense and defense stalled. Thacker fouled out, while Bonham and Cincy's point guard Tony Yates each had 4 fouls. Many of those fouls were called as they tried to stop Stallworth throughout the game. Both Cincy players tightened up because they were in foul trouble.

Dave and the rest of the team took advantage of Cincy's hesitancy. With some key plays made by other team members, especially a steal with one minute left by senior reserve Jim Maddox that allowed Stallworth to hit a shot to bring the Shocks within one. Dave closed out the game at the end with two free throws, putting the Shocks over the top, 65-64. As the clock ran out, the Roundhouse went nuts. It was a madhouse on the floor after the game, as if the Shocks had won the national championship.

In a way, they kind of did because two weeks later, the Shockers upset Loyola of Chicago on its home court by one point. As noted in the last chapter, Cincy met Loyola in the NCAA title game three weeks later and lost an overtime game they should have won, again blowing a lead near the end of the game as they did against the Shockers. With Stallworth leading the way, the Shockers had thus beaten *both* title team games that same year.

Amazingly enough, Dave didn't even consider the Cincy performance his best of that year. When Dave was asked by the *Wichita Beacon* before his last two college games, what *he* thought was his greatest game, it was *not* the Cincy spectacular. Stallworth cited instead as his best his 38 point-16 rebound-8 assist performance, with "great defense" in the Shockers' 79-60 win over Bradley that year.

OK, Dave, you're entitled to your opinion. We suspect those who were at the Cincy game would beg to differ.

One of them was a young man then in his early 20s who had been recruited by Coach Miller, on the strength of a recommendation from Lanny Van Eman, to come to Wichita to help Miller recruit more basketball players from the Pennsylvania pipeline. He was at the Cincy game and literally fell over the seat in front of him after the Shockers won.

His name was Sonny Vaccaro, who would go on to have a "you-can't-believe-it" life story, once featured on ESPN's 30 for 30 ("Sole Man") and again to be the focus of a motion picture to be released in the winter of 2022. With Hollywood star Matt Damon playing Vaccaro, alongside a host of other Hollywood stars (including Ben Affleck) in the movie. His autobiography should also be coming out shortly after this book is published, and readers can learn there about his remarkable life story.

Most famously, Sonny was once the Nike executive who persuaded Nike founder Phil Knight to sign Michael Jordan – yes, the basketball GOAT in the view of many – to the shoe contract that would lead to "Air Jordans". Sonny spent about a decade traveling with MJ, so he knows a thing or two about basketball greatness. Sonny told us that watching Stallworth that night was one of the "top ten sports experiences of his life."

Many, maybe most of those in the Roundhouse that February night, would agree. Including one of the co-authors of this book, whose journey from that night in a roundabout way led to the two authors' friendship and the writing of this book. Readers will discover how later in this book.

# Chapter Four: Dave and the Shockers Come Oh So Close

As the 1963-64 season opened, the Shocks were poised to make some real national noise, clearly capable of winning the Missouri Valley title and finally going to the NCAA tournament.

Stallworth, Bowman, and Leach were coming back, along with the superb senior backcourt, Leonard Kelley and Ernie Moore. Although Kelley was scheduled to graduate mid-season, the Shockers had another guard-phenom-to-be from Wichita East, sophomore Kelly Pete (who later in adulthood would change his name to Mohammed Sharif) and sophomore John Criss from Wichita State Southeast (and a rival of Pete's since their 7th grade) ready to replace them in the season's second half. All four guards were outstanding shooters and great defenders, though Shocker fans will forever debate whether Kelley's and Moore's absence in the post-season cost the Shocks' chances to go all the way.

The bench was strong, too, with some players who could provide some useful minutes and who, in the following year, would make some even more important contributions: 6' 4" junior forward Vernon Smith, 6'7" junior center Larry Nosich, and 6' 9" center, Gerald Davis.

The team and its avid fans couldn't wait for the real season to begin.

\*\*\*

This was also the first season on the campus of your former Shocker co-author, Bob Powers, another Pittsburgh area import (Washington, Pennsylvania) recruited by Lanny Van Eman. From here through chapter 8, unless we say otherwise, the "I" is Powers' writing in the first person and the "we" refers to the '63-'64 team.

I was 6' 8" and, if I say so myself, pretty tough. I weighed about 240 pounds, all muscle from running on the beach during the summers, lifeguarding near Atlantic City, and rowing in all the south Jersey lifeboat races up and down the south Jersey coast.

I never dreamed of playing college basketball. In my sophomore year, a coach walked past the schoolyard court one day at lunchtime. The coach must have been impressed with my size. "What's your name," he asked. "Powers," I said. "You want to play on this high school team?" he asked. I told him I didn't know anything about the game. His short answer: "I will teach you."

I never looked back. In the winter, I played basketball anywhere I could find a game. Indoors, outdoors didn't matter. We would even drive to play pickup games well into the southwestern Pennsylvania hills, poverty all around because that's where some of the best players in the state lived. We played on *dirt courts.* With "baskets" of wire hoops on telephone poles. Often at night, maybe one streetlight in the distance gives us a bit of light. We played late into the night, then drove home soaking wet with sweat dripping from our bodies.

Between my summers rowing and winters playing basketball, my life was perfect. My basketball game also benefitted from my playing with and against my more basketball talented 6' 6" brother, Steve, who was a star on VMI's basketball team. He also threw the javelin on the track team.

To my surprise, my high coach Ray Natali started receiving letters from college coaches. Rowing and basketball scholarships were there for the picking. I wanted to go to college on a rowing scholarship. If I say so myself, I was a great singles oarsman. I loved and continue to love that sport.

The problem for me was that the entrance requirements to the schools that offered rowing scholarships were way above my "academic" pay grade. Wisconsin was offering me a full rowing scholarship. I wanted to go there so badly. It was not to be. However, my recruiting visit to Wichita left one big impression and involved one harrowing moment. After Lanny picked me up at the airport, and as we drove north to 17$^{th}$ street towards the University, he pointed out the poorest sections of Wichita. I immediately thought, "this is nothing compared to the poor areas I grew up in." Pittsburgh, Philadelphia and Atlantic City – all places I frequented in my youth – had *real* poverty.

The harrowing moment came the next day. Johnny Criss was the student-athlete who got the $20 to escort me around campus and the city. On that first morning, we went to Fairmount Park behind Brennan Hall, off 17$^{th}$ street. Bowman, Pete and Stallworth were waiting for me. "How about a little 2 on 2, Bob?"

I had no basketball shoes. One of them grabbed a pair of extra Chuck Taylors they brought along just in case. These fellas were cut and ready to play. No small talk, I just got right into it. First time in my life, I was in a pick-up game where I felt like everything was on the line. I had not yet signed my letter of intent, so I was really nervous. I wasn't sure if this was my try-out or not.

I must have passed the test because Johnny introduced me to the rest of the team as the weekend passed. Every team member was a gentleman. I asked questions about how tough the classes and professors were. They assured me that the team members had personal tutors for any subject where I felt I needed the extra help. Before I left, I got an offer from Coach Miller to join the team.

My mind raced on the plane ride back to Pennsylvania. I had to decide between three schools that were recruiting me. My parents did not have the college experience to counsel me, so they sent me to our pastor. His exact words, "follow your gut, Bob. Always, you will never go wrong."

My gut told me Wichita is where I ought to go, even though before my Wichita recruitment and campus visit, I had barely heard of the place. Being a small-town kid from Little Washington, Pennsylvania, I spelled Wichita with an "h" — Whichita. I was expecting cowboys with horses tied up in the streets.

In the end, here's how I decided. Our father ran our home like a Marine Corps barracks. Don't get me wrong; he was a loving dad. But still, pretty tough. So, when I got the basketball scholarship offer to play in Wichita, Kansas — a long way from Washington, Pennsylvania — I jumped at the opportunity to leave home.

It was a huge adjustment, but I made it (as most college students do). My new roommate from Pittsburg, Kansas -- up until then, I thought there was only *one* Pittsburgh, and it was *not* in Kanas — told me the Indians would come down from the hills to the drive-in theaters, put speakers on the horns of their saddles, sit on the ground and then watch the movie. I did not question any of the stories until later. It shows you my naivete, at least at the beginning.

My recruiting class of 1963, with 12 freshmen on scholarship, at the time, was the largest freshman team in Wichita University's history. Many were very talented. However, Tommy Newman, Melvin Reed, Al Trope, Jamie Thompson, and I were the only five chosen to move into our sophomore year together. I was amazed that I made the cut.

One who didn't even get that far was Phil Anderson from Laguna Beach, CA. His expertise was surfing and volleyball. That boy could jump! My being an oarsman gave us a common ground to buddy up. However, it didn't take long before his need to be on the beach overwhelmed him. Phil was gone at mid-semester of our freshman year.

Our freshman games typically started at 5:45 pm, right before the varsity games at 8 pm. In high school, we had 200-300 in the stands. In 1963, by 6:15, Henry Levitt was filling up for the varsity game. In the last quarter of our freshman games, we had over 7,000 people watching us play. That's because our varsity team was a powerhouse, driven largely by Stallworth. It was awesome to play in front of that many fans. I never saw anything like it. The whole fieldhouse would be filled with smoke. In those days, nobody cared.

In 1963 the University of Wichita's enrollment was 6,700 students. A year later, Wichita became a state school, and our name changed to Wichita State University, with 10,800 students. With a much larger student body and a top-of-the-line fieldhouse, Henry Levitt Arena, we were primed to hit the big time. Little did we know that this basketball team with players from all over the USA would make history for our school and city.

\*\*\*

Dave Stallworth was a second-semester junior during my freshman year. I only got to play with him for 18 months. I learned the most about him during my freshman year when all I could do was practice against him every day. He was like a cat or even a ghost on the floor.

You get hard fast when you regularly play against a group of men this fierce every day. The assistant coaches — Ron Heller and Gary Thompson (both former Shocker standouts) — were always on the practice floor, watching all our moves, up close and personal. Ralph was in the stands sucking on those non-filter camels and barking out orders. "Powers, you push Bowman one more time, and I will buy you a one-way ticket back to that place you call home!" He didn't care that Nate, with his huge wingspan and elbows sticking out and hitting me in the jaw, was not just a big obstacle, but he hurt! No wonder I shoved him now and then.

Dave's game on the court mirrored his personality. He never got upset on the floor. Instead, he took it all out on whoever was guarding him. You could tell when he was ready to retaliate. He could destroy any of us like we were a fly on the wall. You tried to be your best against him but not provoke him to crush you.

Not many teams the Shocker varsity played against that year were any more successful than our freshman team was in practice. The Shockers had a great regular season at 21-5, with a 10-2 MVC record, notching first place in the Valley.

Dave averaged 26 points and over 10 rebounds a game. Dave had plenty of company on that Shocker team. Nate Bowman added nearly 13 per game, with 9 rebounds. Ernie Moore, Leonard Kelley and Kelly Pete added 17, 11 and 9, respectively. It was a powerhouse team, ranked 5$^{th}$ in the country, and having won the Valley, we were finally heading to the NCAA tournament in March 1964.

***

But not before winning some memorable regular season games. At the top of the list was our away game at Cincinnati, the team we had upset the previous year at the

Roundhouse and also beat at the Roundhouse rematch on January 30, 1964.

Still, we hadn't beaten Cincy on their court since Lanny Van Eman's buzzer-beater jump shot that gave the Shockers a 52-51 win in December 1961, stopping the second-ranked Cincy's 27-game winning streak at that time. The away game at Cincy came just a little more than two weeks after the earlier Roundhouse win. We were ranked 6$^{th}$ in the country at the time.

The game was nip and tuck throughout. As he had done on other occasions, Dave hit the apparent game-winner, after Ernie Moore stole the ball with 45 seconds left, to put the Shocks up 56-54. The team ran off the court and was celebrating in the locker room, many taking showers, when Coach Miller came in and said we had to return to the court because the timekeeper had ruled that Dave's last-second shot didn't count – even though he got it off before the gun fired. Games weren't officially over in those days until a gun (using blanks) went off. Seriously. The timekeeper also could overrule the refs on the floor, and that's what they did (today, of course, the refs would review the video, and *they* would make final rulings).

Amazingly, our varsity team didn't let this bit of misfortune keep them from winning in overtime, which they did by one point after Dave Stallworth put a missed Nate Bowman free throwback in the basket. His teammate Dave Leach said many years later, "We were determined they weren't going to get that one from us," Leach said. "We thought we had already won. Dave carried us the rest of the way."

Miller recalls in his book that 10,000 fans greeted the team at the airport when they returned home. Paul Suellentrop, the Shocker's current journalist-in-residence, reports on a Shocker website a lower estimate of 2,000. But who's counting? Suellentrop adds that the airline that flew the team back, Braniff Airways (remember them!), presented the Shockers with a trophy saying "One Game-Won Twice", reflecting the two "winning" scores, 56-54 and 59-58.

Incidentally, the practice of Shocker fans showing up at the airport to greet the team coming back – or to send them off – has continued through the years. Fans showing up that way was routine when I was playing.

Miller tells another story in his autobiography about that game in his book. In those days, away games were not televised live. The Cincy game was shown the next day after Miller had already returned. In watching the game the next day with his wife, Jean, Miller apparently got very worked up all over again about the apparent theft of the game by the refs. Jean told him: "Settle down, Ralph. There's no reason to get upset. We're going to win, anyway." Jean must have been one of the only people who could talk to Coach Miller like that!

Cincy may have gotten the last laugh, though. The Shockers wouldn't win at Cincy again for another 54 years, not until 2018.

\*\*\*

We also had a few disappointing regular season losses, especially two at the beginning of the season, which we opened with a 5$^{th}$ place national ranking. A one-point loss in the first month of play at Texas Western, followed several days later by a six-point loss at Arizona State, where Dave's 43 points were not enough to put the Shockers over the top.

Texas Western, basketball fans know, won the national championship several years later, in the 1965-66 season, the first school with an all-black starting lineup to do so. It turns out that Ralph Miller also used an all-black starting lineup earlier at Wichita..

There was Another Wichita-Texas Western connection: Lanny had recruited Texas Western's star center, David Lattin, or "Big Daddy D", to come to Wichita, but Lattin chose Texas Western instead. Turned out alright for him. He and his teammates won the national championship against an all-white team from Kentucky, which had a star guard named Pat Riley. Yes, that Pat Riley! The movie *Glory Road*, one of the best sports movies around, depicts the struggles Texas Western surmounted to get to college basketball's moIn any event, we still had to win a "play-in" game against Drake to qualify for the NCAA tournament. That's because our two teams were tied at season's end for first, with 10-2 records. We won that game 58-50, and for the first time in Miller's career and in school history, we went to the NCAA tournament.

By good fortune, the regional was held in the Roundhouse, our home court that year! So, we had a lot of confidence that we could win two games at home and move on to the Final Four, which waaheld that year in Kansas City's old Municipal Auditorium. In an interview for this book, Lanny told us that he had already been sent west to scout the regional there so the Shocks would be prepared for the winner once they got to Kansas City.

As it turned out, overconfidence did us in. Because after easily winning our first game against Creighton (which was led that year by the great Paul Silas) by 16 points, we lost to another Kansas team, Kansas State, in the regional final, 94-86, in a hard-fought, well-played game. The Shockers were hobbled by three fouls called on Stallworth and two on Bowman in the first half, which didn't stop Stallworth from making 25 of his 37 points in the second half. Although Coach Miller said the team played as well as it could, K State was hot and simply played better. Our loss to K State was a bitter disappointment, especially because we had been playing so well up until that point.

Many years later, writing in his autobiography, Ralph Miller still had no doubt we would have "won" – though it is not clear whether he was referring to that regional final or to the entire tournament –if we had had Ernie Moore playing in the post-season. To Tommy Newman, a freshman that year, the reference couldn't have been clearer: it was the *national championship* the team could have earned. The Shockers didn't have Moore for the post-season because Ernie was academically ineligible earlier in his career. Due to what Miller called a "technicality", Ernie was therefore eligible only for conference games at the end of the regular season but not for the NCAA tournament.

That year, UCLA won the national championship, beating K St in the national semifinal and then besting Duke in the final. The Bruins' win would begin the school's amazing streak of winning the national championship 10 times out of 12 years, all under the great Coach John

Wooden. By an amazing turn of events, the Shockers would meet UCLA the following year in the national semifinal, but without Dave. Shocker fans of that era know the reason why, and readers will too when they turn to the next chapter.

Speaking of the next chapters, at the close of the 1963-64 season, Coach Miller had a surprising one of his own. He left Wichita to coach Iowa. It was a "shocker" to us all, to say the least. We suspected that Coach got a better financial deal from Iowa, but still, it was a surprise that he left us, even as hard as he was on us on many occasions. We'll never know, but maybe that loss to K St also had something to do with his decision.

My first impression of Wichita was in 1963 when Coach Van Eman called to offer me a full scholarship to attend the University of Wichita.

# Chapter Five: Dave's Final "Half" Season

I was excited to return to school as a sophomore for the 1965-66 season because I had made it to the varsity!

But the entire team also had mixed feelings about the coming season. That is because we all knew that Dave would be graduating mid-season and leaving us.

Even before he left for Iowa, Ralph Miller did the best he could to prepare for that eventuality the season before by scheduling our toughest road games in the first half of the season. That way, the team without Dave at least would have a fighting chance to repeat as conference champions. What Miller and none of us could anticipate is that in mid-season, we would also lose our anchor in the center, Nate Bowman, who didn't pass an anthropology course that first semester. That made him ineligible for the second half of the season. Yet, miracles or near miracles sometimes happen. We get to that story in the next chapter.

Miller's assistant, Gary Thompson, was the new coach and widely liked as a "players' coach". He also could and did take advantage of Miller's systems in practice and on the floor during games.

***

The 1964-65 season itself was like a Tale of Two Cities. More than the first half of the season – 16 games to be precise – constituted Dave's last eligible semester. He made the most of it, averaging 25 points, over 12 rebounds, and nearly 6 assists per game.

Playing a tough pre-conference and conference schedule, the team had a 13-3 overall record and was undefeated in the Valley at 6-0, when Dave had to bow out.

One game in the first half of the season stands out. December 14, 1964. At Detroit's famed Cobo stadium, then the home of the Detroit Pistons, but opened for our game against Michigan. We were ranked number one, with Dave our star. The Wolverines were ranked second, led by their All-American Cazzie Russell. It was that year's basketball "Game of the Century". And it lived up to its billing.

Despite Dave having had an off-night – he only scored 11 points due to Michigan's tough on and off zone defense deployed against him – the Shockers fought the Wolverines toe-to-toe until the very end. Nate Bowman and Dave Leach had great games, with 24 and 23 points, respectively. Leach, in particular, was highly effective shooting over the zone, precisely what Michigan feared. Over the entire gamee, the Shockers shot 59 percent from the field, better than Michigan's 55 percent.

With the game tied, we had the ball with 28 seconds to go and, remember, no shot clock. Knowing that Thompson had the team stall, twice calling time out, with the last break coming at seven seconds.

Everyone in the arena, the Wolverines included, expected the ball to be passed into Stallworth, and it was. Dave drove to the basket but dribbled the ball off his foot, which went out of bounds. According to the *Detroit Free Press* account of the game the next day, Cazzie Russell helped to tip the ball off Dave's foot. Many years later, Dave believed that he was fouled, as many Shocker fans do, but it wasn't called. As Dave was quoted, "I never really had a worse moment... I thought I'd get the call even on their court because it was such an obvious foul."

Fate turned. On the next inbound play, with only a few seconds left, the ball went to Cazzie's teammate George Pomey, who quickly passed it to Cazzie at mid-court. Russell took two dribbles, then heaved it... over John Criss' outstretched hand (which he remembers to this day)... and it went in. Michigan 87-85. The 11,000-plus fans in Cobo went wild.

Cazzie had 28 points that night, 23 in the second half. He would go on to be the first pick in the 1966 NBA draft by the Knicks, who took Stallworth as the third overall pick at the end of the 1965 season. Both would play as teammates alongside Princeton's Bill Bradley, who was also picked by the Knicks in 1965 but didn't join them for two years until after he completed his Rhodes scholarship in England. More about "Dollar Bill", as he was widely called at the time, later.

Dave and Cazzie relived that Michigan game even as pros. The *Detroit Free Press* said about the game the next day: "There may have been basketball games as good, but never one better."

The last two games of Dave's college career were especially memorable. The first was an away game on January 29, 1965, at Loyola, the NCAA champ from the previous year. This is the game that Coach K, who has kindly written a jacket endorsement for this book, attended as a teenager and saw Dave in person.

The 13,000-plus Chicago crowd was treated to a nail-biter, which was tied at the end of regulation play, 83-83. In the overtime, Gerald Davis put the Shockers ahead by one point with a free throw with ten seconds to go. But after a missed shot with time in OT winding down, Loyola's Tom Markey put it up again for a one-point win, 93-92. Stallworth was magnificent, scoring 45 points, two of them at the 20-second mark in OT, which tied the game then.

It was a bitter loss for the Shockers, who led by nine at halftime. But foul trouble for Kelly Pete and Vernon Smith – who together would play critical roles in the team's success after Dave's departure – kept them out of enough of the second half to allow Loyola to catch up and put the game into overtime.

Dave played his final game the very next night. Fittingly, it was at the Roundhouse against Louisville, which going into the game was 4-2 in the Valley. The contest wasn't close, a 97-76 blowout for the Shockers, who clearly were amped up and not about to let Stallworth leave on a loss. Dave obliged, nabbing 15 rebounds and scoring 40 points on an array of shots that Mike Kennedy has told others and us was as dazzling as anything he has ever seen.

The packed Roundhouse of almost 10,500 fans gave standing ovations to Dave before and after the game. He was feted with a ceremony celebrating his incomparable four years as a Shocker.

Although I didn't get into any games while Dave was there, riding that bench my sophomore year was the greatest experience of my life. After the games, I would tell the guys we had the best seats in the house. I will never forget those days. Watching David Stallworth play up close and personal was one of the highlights of my life.

Dave Leach

Academic All-American & Team Captain

Head Coach Gary Thompson with son Cory and Dave after a 20-minute standing ovation for Dave'd last Shocker career home game 1964 in the Fieldhouse

# Chapter Six: Our Near Miracle

There's a saying in sports when one player gets injured or, in some other way, can't play: Next Man Up. It's the Next Man Up mentality that drives championship teams to do remarkable things when one or more of their best players goes down.

We all knew that we'd need that Next Man Up mentality when Dave graduated for the rest of the season. But we were not prepared for having to double it, meaning Next *Two* Men up. That's because Nate was declared ineligible for the rest of the season when it was announced in late January that he had failed that anthropology exam.

There was a silver lining, if you can call it that, to losing both Dave and Nate. The rest of the team had to grow up quickly, with a lot on the line. And remarkably, that's exactly what we did. Much of that can be attributed to our coach, Gary Thompson, who believed we could pull off a miracle by winning the Missouri Valley Conference again, which is what happened, though not without some difficulty.

But a lot of our subsequent success that season can be attributed to the inspiration and winning mentality that Dave gave us while he was the leader of the team. And so that's why it's fitting in a book about Dave to remind readers of his immediate legacy – the confidence he gave the rest of the team to do things we probably never thought possible.

Before retelling the story of that miracle second half of the season, we want to pause to let readers know who these guys were that pulled it off.

\*\*\*

We have already mentioned Dave Leach several times. He had played with the "other" Dave – Stallworth -- for two and a half years. Leach was really a wing forward with a deadly shot from the corner. So deadly that both corners on our side of the court came to be known as "Leach's Alley". But with Nate no longer at the center, Dave was the tallest starter left, so by default, he became our undersized center at 6' 5" for the rest of the season. A pretty remarkable story given that Wichita was the only major university to recruit Leach, who played his high school ball in McPherson, Kansas (the same town where my co-author Bob Litan spent the first five years of his life).

Leach was a great leader on and off the court. An excellent student, he was named an Academic All-American. Dave was also president of his senior class. He would go on after graduation to become a successful high school coach in Wichita, then an assistant to Coach Miller at Oregon State, before becoming the head coach at Boise

State. After coaching, Dave became a successful financial consultant, handling, among other accounts, that of Coach Miller.

Our floor leader from the first half of the season, junior Kelly Pete, would be asked to become an even more important part of the team in the second half. He answered that call. Although 6' 1", Kelly was a great leaper and scorer and would guard taller opposing players with his tenacious defense throughout the rest of the season. When he graduated the following year, Kelly was the fourth leading scorer in Shocker history.

Kelly, who later changed his name to Mohamad Sharif, eventually moved to Santa Fe, Mexico, where he became a dealer and collector of African art. He was not the only Shocker with an eye for art. As we noted earlier, after his NBA career, Gene Wiley turned his youthful artistic talent into a career as a professional artist.

Jamie Thompson, who would become one of the best shooters in Shocker history, then was just a sophomore and played at the guard position in the first half of the season. That all changed in the second half when he was slotted in the starting lineup as an undersized forward at 6"3" (hell, virtually all the starters were undersized at their positions after Dave and Nate left!). Coach Gary Thompson didn't really have another choice.

Jamie more than seized his opportunity. He became one of the team's leading scorers in the second half of the season, culminating in his 36 points in the national semifinal (more about that soon). Even into his 40s and 50s, Jamie was "the man" at pickup games in Las Vegas, playing with and competing at the level of the NBA stars who would show up. Jamie, a great golfer too who grew up across from the MacDonald's public golf course in Wichita, left us too early, dying of a heart attack in 2006.

Vernon Smith, a senior and our other starting forward at 6' 4", stepped up in the second half of the season to have some big games for us in the post-season NCAA tournament. Vernon, a native of Newton, just 20 miles north of Wichita, started his college playing career at Oklahoma State before transferring to Wichita. Vernon would have one of his greatest games against the Cowboys in the post-season.

After graduation from the army, Vernon had a long career as a high school guidance counselor in California. Like many other basketball players, the sports gene runs in the Smith family. Vernon and his wife had two daughters, both athletes: one in track at Oregon, the other in volleyball at Oregon State (where she played on the "Ralph Miller" basketball court). Vernon's granddaughter Claire is a two-time all-American volleyball star at the University of Washington.

As a starter, Johnny Criss, our 5'10" junior guard, also stepped up big-time in the second half of the season. Johnnie was a deadly shooter who often was open on assists from Kelly, his one-time high school rival. Johnny also lettered in baseball at Wichita, as did his son Matt. After graduation, Criss coached high school basketball, was coach of the Shocker freshman team, and later head basketball coach at Coffeyville Community College.

Gerald Davis, at 6' 9" from Brooklyn, New York, was Leach's backup at the center as a junior. He played in 24 of the Shockers' games that season, including three of our four post-season games. Gerry was the quiet type, also cerebral. He carried himself with dignity, off and on the court. After graduation, Gerry spent many years in law enforcement, retiring as a parole officer in New York City.

Melvin Reed, a 6' 5" sophomore from Dallas, Texas, had played against both Stallworth and Bowman in high school and followed them to Wichita. He also played backup center in the 1964-65 season and, in subsequent years, was a starter at that position. His athletic skills – he was the Missouri

Valley high jump champion twice –more than made up for his size.

Larry Nosich, a 6' 7" senior center, was part of the McKeesport pipeline but an unconventional recruit to say the least. Larry didn't play high school basketball because the school he attended was so far from his home. Instead, he worked for six years after graduating high school in a steel mill, playing recreational basketball in the evenings. Lanny saw him play, and by a stroke of luck (his words), at the age of 24, he received an athletic scholarship to play at Wichita.

Larry played in most of the Shocker games, especially after Dave and Nate left, during that memorable 1964-65 season. After graduation, he returned to a better job at the same steel mill where he had worked. Eventually, he was promoted to management, which he says would never have happened without that scholarship and the degree he earned from Wichita University.

Tommy Newman, listed as a 6' 1" sophomore guard (but in his own telling, a shade under 6') from Ft. Worth, Texas, had an excellent freshman year and probably would have played a good deal in the 1964-65 season. But Tommy tore his ACL in his knee in a preseason practice session, and though he tried to play through it early in the season, he and the coaches decided it would be best for him to redshirt and rehab. So, Tommy could only watch his teammates during that amazing season from the sidelines.

Tommy's injury also limited his playing time in his following two years at Wichita. He didn't come back to play his final "redshirt" year, but in a move for which he always has been grateful, Coach Thompson asked Tommy if he would like to coach the Shockers' freshman team. That put Newman on his way to a legendary high school coaching career in Texas, where he was inducted into the Texas high school basketball Hall of Fame in 2000. He also was an assistant coach at Baylor and head coach at Texas Wesleyan, North Texas.

Then there were the bench riders along with me, who also got some sporadic game time as well. But these guys pushed the varsity every day in practice to be as successful as they became. 6' 8" Gerry Reimond, 6' 7" Al Trope, and 5' 11" Manny Zefiros.

Gerry, part of the Pennsylvania pipeline recruited by Lanny Eman, became a successful investment banker after graduation. Al has had a successful business career. After graduation, Manny became a highly successful tennis coach. His son Jason was a tennis star at Arizona and Florida State.

\*\*\*

Our first game without Dave and Nate was against St. Louis at the Roundhouse. A tough opponent, they were 4-2 at the time, not that far behind us in the MVC standings. St. Louis had a tall front line that would be matched up against Leach, our new undersized center, and Vernon Smith, really a small forward. The Shockers nonetheless proved the doubters wrong. Leach played great defense, while Kelly Pete scored 23 and Thompson added another 21, enough to give the Shockers a 72-64 win.

With a 7-0 MVC record after that, we barely hung on -- surviving losses to Bradley, Tulsa, and Louisville -- the rest of the season to win the conference title again, all without Dave and Nate.

That's because a lot of players continued to step up. Jamie Thompson went from being an obscure role player to our leading scorer. Kelly Pete was a magician at point guard and always our most ferocious defender. Dave Leach seamlessly moved from his forward position to playing routinely against much larger centers. And the rest of our players did their jobs when they were called on to do so.

The last regular season game at home against Drake was a nail-biting 76-74 overtime win that clinched the MVC title, which meant the Shocks were headed for the NCAA tournament for the second year in a row. In an ironic twist, we would play our first tournament game in Manhattan, Kansas, the home of Kansas State, which ended the Shockers' season the year before in the regional finals.

Going into the tournament, few gave us a chance to survive, even the first game against SMU, let alone make it to the Final Four. But as Al Michaels famously asked after the USA Hockey team beat the Russians in the 1980 Olympics – "Do you believe in miracles?" – that's exactly what our team believed, and then went out and executed.

That's not the way the SMU game started, though. The Shocks were quickly down 7 and trailed by 10 with six minutes to go before halftime. Then we put on a full-court press, led by our defensive stopper, Kelly Pete, and forced some turnovers. Three minutes later, we tied the game.

Our two teams see-sawed through the rest of the game, with the Shockers' press keeping us close. SMU's coach Doc Hayes was quoted in the *Eagle* the next day, "We had never seen anything like it before." But even with the press, the Shocks needed more when Pete and Leach were benched for a good portion of the second half with foul trouble.

That's when our bench, led by Melvin Reed's 7 points and Gerald Davis' defense, saved the day, going into a "ball control" offense that slowed the game until late when Leach and Pete could return. That strategy wouldn't work today with the shot clock in place. But in those days, ball control helped us when we needed it. We squeaked through with an 86-81 win, with Kelly scoring a critical 3 points near the end, giving him a game-high of 31.

The SMU win put us in the next night's regional final against Oklahoma State. The Cowboys' legendary coach, Henry "Hank" Iba, was coaching his final season, which may have put some added pressure on his team that didn't need it. Still, we were the underdogs, though we had an estimated 5,000 of our fans in attendance. Lanny and Ralph both came back to witness the game (they could have been coaching in that game had they not gone to Iowa!).

Iba was known for the ball control style of play of his teams. That is precisely how the Cowboys played in that final. Against most teams, which played more up-tempo, Iba's approach worked because it frustrated these opponents. But it was the wrong way to play against us since we had learned to play ball control ourselves as a way of offsetting our size disadvantage.

So that's why we were able to turn the tables against the Cowboys. Kelly Pete led the way with 19 points. Vernon Smith played an outstanding game with 12 points against his former team. Leach was a rock at center with 11. Jamie added 7, and Jonny Criss came through with 5. All clutch buckets. Enough to win, 56-46, in a slow-it-down, hard-nosed defensive game.

Amazingly, all five Shocker starters – all playing in high school within a 60-mile radius of Wichita – played the whole game. No subs. The *Eagle* called them the "Iron Men" the next day.

With our improbable win in the regional final, we headed to Portland, Oregon, to play in the national semifinal against UCLA. We were the Cinderella team of the tournament, again up against long odds. But not impossible. After all, earlier in the season, UCLA had lost to Ralph Miller's Iowa team in Chicago in the same doubleheader at Chicago Stadium where we had barely lost to Loyola (though with Dave Stallworth in his next-to-last game). Moreover, despite having the best backcourt in college basketball – with all-Americans Gail Goodrich and Keith Erickson – the Bruins didn't have the kind of size that other teams had used against us in the second half of the season. Still, the Bruins were the defending national champs, and they had that dreaded fast break, along with a pressing full-court defense, modeled somewhat (though refined) on Ralph Miller's 2-2-1.

Our Cinderella moment didn't last long. We had it tied at 13-13 early in the game, but then the Bruins ran away with the game after that. They were up by 27 at halftime, ultimately triumphing at 108-89. There was one bright spot for the Shockers. Jamie Thompson's incredible shooting, 13 for 19 from the floor, with a game-high total of 36. Jamie showed off the shooting talent he would display for the rest of his Shocker career.

In those days, the NCAA Final Four conducted a consolation game before the title game, that year pitting UCLA against the Michigan team that had beaten us, barely, early in the season. UCLA won that game, clinching its second of its many national championships.

Our consolation game was another blowout loss for us, this time against the Ivy League champs, Princeton. The Tigers were led by arguably the best basketball player in the country, Bill Bradley, who later would become a teammate of Dave Stallworth's with the New York Knicks (see Chapter 9). We were trounced by 118-82, an even worse loss than UCLA's previous night's drubbing.

NCAA consolation games ordinarily are never remembered by anyone. Not our loss to Princeton. That night, Bradley put on a phenomenal performance, hitting 22 of 29 from the field and 14 of 15 from the line, on his way to a record 58 point game. Reportedly, during the game, Princeton's coach Bill Van Breda Kolff (who would later go on to coach the Los Angeles Lakers) had to push Bradley, who was also a great passer, to keep shooting because he was so hot. Yikes!

Many years later, I invited Bradley to come to the 50$^{th}$ reunion of that 1964-65 season. Although he politely declined, he wrote about that night (the letter itself appears later): "The baskets were good to me that night. What you might not have known is that we installed a basketball magnet invented in a Princeton lab. Its effect was to pull the ball into the basket. And you just thought I shot well." He is one class act.

Although the outcomes of the two Final Four games were disappointing, it was a huge achievement that the Shockers even made it that far. Shocker fans since have fantasized how different the outcomes would have been had Nate been able to play, let alone Stallworth.

***

What happened in the second half of that unforgettable 1964-65 season couldn't have been accomplished without the firm but the gentle guiding hand of our coach Gary Thompson. After a stellar high school sports record – in football, basketball, baseball, and track – Gary was recruited by Ralph Miller to play guard on his first Wichita State team in the early 1950s. After service in the army, Gary was asked by Ralph Miller to be his assistant, which he was for seven years before being picked to be his replacement.

The 1964-65 season was the zenith of Gary's coaching career, which lasted for seven years at Wichita State. After coaching, Thompson became financially successful as a Pizza Hut franchisee, as did many others in Wichita and around the country. Gary died too soon in 2010.

Gary's wife Betty, with whom he shared 65 years of dating and then marriage, recalled how much good sportsmanship mattered to Gary and how he lived it (see her notes at the end of the chapter). Two examples from that remarkable 1964-65 post-season stand out.

One is that although Gary clearly was elated by the win over Oklahoma State, he truly felt bad for the Cowboys' coach, the legendary Hank Iba. Gary greatly respected Iba and knew this game would be the last of Iba's long career. Gary told Iba how he felt.

The other example came from Princeton's trouncing of the Shockers in the national consolation game when Bradley put up those 58 points. As Bradley continued to make basket after basket, Gary became awestruck at what he was witnessing – clearly no different than the reaction of those watching in the arena. Toward the end, Gary began clapping at every shot Bradley made. He never did that again with any opposing player for the rest of his coaching career.

---

Congratulations to the team. Spouses, fans and all of you who put this celebration together. What a wonderful tribute to Dave in appreciation for all he accomplished. He put WU-WSU on the map. Sportswise.. I am sorry I am not able to be there. Cory and Karen will be there - representing the Gary Thompson family

Mrs Coach Thompson

A special hello and thank you to
Gregg and Lynn Marshall
Gloria Stallworth
and
Ann and Bruce LaRose

— Betty

and Bob Powers for his organization skills!

---

Betty's notes to our team.

Sept 20, 2018

Re David Stallworth Memo

"ALWAYS REMEMBER FROM WHENCE YOU CAME" JIMMY V

Dear Bob,

Can you put this card and note some where to be seen? I'm sorry I can't be with you for the celebration. I will be thinking of all of you.

Best regards —
Betty

P.S. Could you please send me a copy of the basket- ball schedule? No Fred — no Ron — no Conner, no Shag- no Landry, no Austin — who will replace them???

To clarify Bradley's scribble.

**BILL BRADELY**

1/5/15

Dear Robert-

It's hard to believe that it's been 50 years since we met in the final four in Portland. The baskets were good to me that night. What you might not have known is that we installed a basketball magnet invented in a Princeton lab. It's effect was to pull the ball into the basket. And you thought I just shot well - seriously. I wish you well with the reunion. The Princeton team has our reunion March 7th.
I will give them your regards -
Thanks and best wishes

Bill Bradely

**BILL BRADLEY**

1/5/15

Dear Robert –

It's hard to believe that it's been 50 years since we met in the final four in Portland. The baskets were good to me that night. What you might not have known is that we installed a basketball magnet, invented in a Princeton lab. It's effect was to pull the ball into the basket. And you thought I just shot well – Seriously I wish you well with the reunion. The Princeton team has our reunion March 7th. I will give them your regards –

Thanks & Best Wishes

Bill Brdly

The 1964-65 Team

Dave Stallworth 42

Middle Second Row

40th reunion of the 1964-65 team

Tall Grass Country Club

Tommy Newman was missing to accept his induction into the Texas Basketball Hall of Fame

# Chapter Seven: Dave On and Off the Court

As teammates, we all knew Dave almost entirely from our daily practices and, of course, playing with or watching him at games. Except for Nate, who hung out with Dave his first two years on campus, the rest of us didn't spend much time with him off the court. That was especially true after Dave got married his junior year to Judy and moved off campus. Off the court, Dave was a very private person, especially after he was married.

Yet to a man, Dave's teammates have nothing but kind words to say about him as an individual.

Dave himself was kind to everyone on the team, whether or not they started. Manny Zefiros, a 5' 11" guard who came to Wichita from New York and played in just four games during the 1964-65 season, remembers that Dave was one of the first people he met when arriving at his dorm at Wichita. Dave quickly invited him to play with Nate in a local park, treating him as an equal. When Zefiros had doubts about his ability to play on the team, Dave encouraged him to stick it out, which Manny did, and he was able to be part of the Final Four team.

Later, after Dave had joined the Knicks and Manny had returned to New York, Manny saw and spoke with Dave after a few games. When the two of them reunited at the 50$^{th}$ reunion, Dave embraced Manny. Many will never forget Dave's kindness and generosity of spirit.

The one iconic image of Dave that everyone who knew or watched him will always remember is that he was always smiling. Even in intense game situations. Indeed, especially at those times.

Why the smile? Dave told the *Beacon* shortly before his college career ended: "When a player gets mad, he destroys his game, and it's bad for the team. If I get upset, I just smile and try to forget it. *Smiling relaxes me*." If only everyone had such an attitude, in any setting, let alone the craziness of a fast-paced sporting event, the world would be better off.

Dave's teammates also recall that although they remember him to be quiet, he loved to sing. Aretha Franklin. Diana Ross. Mary Wells. A truly happy guy.

***

While his teammates knew that Dave obviously was a great basketball player, few knew how truly athletically talented he really was.

One who did was Dave's close friend during his freshman and sophomore years, Tony Morocco. Tony came to Wichita via the Pittsburgh area pipeline as a fun-loving, free-spirited 6-foot guard who played on the freshman team and for one year on the varsity squad. Tony also roomed with Dave Leach during his freshman year. Unfortunately, Tony's dad had a heart attack during Tony's sophomore year, and he had to return home to finish school.

But he had spent enough time with the basketball team and Stallworth to cumulate many stories. About Dave the athlete. And about Dave as the life of the party.

As we discussed in the opening chapter, Dave was a multi-sport star in high school. He used and showed off his speed in all of them.

Tony reports that Dave could and did run a 10-second hundred-yard dash *with no track training or track shoes.* During fall of 1962, the Arizona State football team came to play the Shockers in football. Arizona State had a remarkable backfield, including Charlie Taylor, who went on to become an all-pro wide receiver with the Washington Redskins, and Henry Carr, who would later set the world record in the 220 yards (200 meters) dash, and win two gold medals at the 1964 Tokyo Olympics.

Somehow, Dave met Carr, and the two got into a good-natured argument about whether Dave could come close to him in the 220. Dave kept insisting that he could. Carr essentially said, "No way." One thing led to another, and a group of students who were there at the time, including Tony, marched to the track surrounding the Wichita football stadium, got some stopwatches, and then watched Dave as he ran the 220 on the track. *In tennis shoes. With essentially no warming up. And, of course, with no formal track training.* Nonetheless, according to Tony, Dave ran the race in something like 22 seconds flat, not far behind Carr's best time in that event of a little under 21 seconds (Carr eventually almost broke the 20-second threshold).

Lanny adds that Dave played golf with just a 3 or 4 handicap after he retired from basketball. And that he was a great swimmer, too.

***

That's not all. Morocco told us that Dave was a great boxer and loved the sport. It certainly helped with his rebounding skills!

Dave's boxing skills relate to another aspect of his personality few, other than his college friends, knew about. Dave could be the life of the party, and when he wanted to, out there, on the edge.

Morocco remembers the time in his freshman dorm when two relatively small, skinny students got into an argument and wanted to box it out. Dave was either there at the time or had heard about it. And so, he took charge, organizing and promoting the boxing match in his own room, where he would also referee. Morocco remembers that while the boxers flailed away, Dave was laughing hard. Others crowded around, making lots of noise. Eventually, the dorm "mother" – Mrs. Rankin – came down and broke up all the fun.

Morocco recalled another occasion when he and Stallworth walked into one of the college's gyms with a balcony and climbing ropes hanging from the ceiling. Stallworth not only climbed high on the ropes but began swinging to and from the balcony – the kind of thing that would have given his basketball coaches heart attacks had they been there to see it. But apparently, a dean found out about all this, and Morocco and Stallworth were kicked out of the gym.

As a young college student, Stallworth acted like a typical college student. He never missed a roadrunner cartoon, was constantly joking, and loved arguing with anyone about sports.

Hijinx aside, Morocco relates this concluding fact about Stallworth. Well after he had returned to the Pittsburgh area, Tony ran into Pittsburgh Steeler Hall of Fame defensive end Dwight White, who died much too soon at the age of 58 in 2006. One of the pillars of the Steeler's "Steel Curtain". In talking with White, Tony learned that White graduated from the same high school, James Madison, eight years after Dave before playing his college football at East Texas State.

Once the James Madison connection was established, White talked 20 minutes non-stop about Stallworth, calling him not just the greatest basketball player to come out of James Madison but the best athlete to come out of that school. This was by one of the greatest defensive football players of all time.

# Chapter Eight: The Ups and the Downs of the College Basketball Life

The team opened the 1965-66 season on an optimistic note. Although Dave Leach had graduated, Melvin Reed replaced him at the center. While Melvin couldn't shoot like Leach – few could – he was very athletic, even at 6' 5," with the jumping ability that made him a high jumping track star as well.

Other key teammates from that 1964-65 miracle team also returned, including Kelly Pete, John Criss, and Jamie Thompson. And with almost as much anticipation as had occurred when Stallworth arrived on campus four years before, Warren Armstrong, the hugely talented and athletic 6' 2" *forward*, was joining the varsity as a sophomore. Armstrong, who would change his name to Warren Jabali, would become a Shocker great and then have a successful pro career in the American Basketball Association (ABA).

And so, not surprisingly, the team did well right out of the gate, winning the first four games of the season, placing us in the top 10 rankings.

Our second game, a rematch with Michigan at the Roundhouse without Stallworth, was one of the season's highlights. Michigan came into the game again ranked second, led by their now senior all-American Russell. Cazzie had 21 that night, but it wasn't enough to overcome an incredible Shocker upset, 100-94. Without our floor leader, Kelly Pete, who couldn't play because of an injured thigh.

Jamie Thompson took the torch instead. Perfect from the field and the line, with 28 points. Guard John Criss was 9 for 10 from the field and scored 19. Melvin Reed, at the center, poured in 16. Lillard Harris, a 5' 11" guard from Ft. Worth, notched 18, and Warren Armstrong added 17.

However, the team's intensity in the Michigan game wore off as the season went on. In our fifth game, we got blown out by Marquette and lost close games to Texas Tech and Bradley. We ended the regular season with a 17-9 record, 9-5 in the Valley, good enough for second. On the strength of that conference record, we were invited back to the NIT but lost our first game, again as in previous years. This time it was to NYU, a local favorite but one without a strong history and tradition of basketball success. The Shockers wouldn't have real luck in the NIT until many years later when the 2010-11 team won the tournament.

***

For me personally, however, my junior year's 1965-66 season didn't start so well. Not playing, aggravated by some injuries in my first two years, started to bother me. I was, after all, the leading rebounder of our freshman team when I also averaged 7 points per game.

Halfway into the season, during a doubleheader trip to Carbondale, Illinois, to play Southern Illinois and then Milwaukee to play Marquette, I had my first major attack of depression. Dave Anderson and I had our room on the 20$^{th}$ floor of the Milwaukee Sheraton hotel. I told Dave, my roommate on that trip that I felt like something crazy was happening inside my head. I wanted to throw a chair through the window in our room and jump out.

Anderson called Gary Thompson, our coach, immediately. Not in his room. Had him paged. He was in the lobby. Dave told him about my condition. Dave took me down the elevator to Gary in the lobby. Gary, let me get it all out of my system. Gary explained that my presence on the practice floor was my real value. That I made it possible for our team to compete against our biggest opponents because of my toughness in practice every day. I was set up for counseling upon our return to Wichita.

After three sessions, the counselor told me I was OK, what had happened in Milwaukee was a one-off, a rare event, and that if I needed to talk again, just to call him. After that episode in Milwaukee, I never felt the same about playing.

I struggled until the end of that season. Each member of the team had an individual meeting with the head coach at the season's end. I told Gary I was packing and heading back to Pennsylvania. Gary's immediate response was, "No, you're not!"

I replied, "I cannot sit on the bench another season. However, neither I nor my folks can pay for me to finish school. I will get a job back home, and everything will be fine."

Gary was insistent: "Bob, you are going to graduate from this university." It almost seemed like he had a personal obligation to finish what his coaching staff had started, especially to my family.

What Gary did later is remarkable, for which I will forever be grateful. He found a way to keep me on scholarship so I could finish up my bachelor's degree. It was life-changing.

***

Back to basketball. Scouting reports and pre-game meals were usually combined to save time. This is what I remember.

For weekend games at home, we'd always check into the Holiday Inn East motel on a Friday night before a Saturday game. I'm sure that was the way our coaches could keep an eye on us, making sure none of us were up to no good before a game, if you know what I mean.

On those occasions, as well as in hotels or motels for away games, we'd have a late breakfast on Saturday mornings. Then a 2 pm meeting in the coaches' suite to review the opposing team's scouting report. We'd get a rundown on each player on the other team, his tendencies, strengths, weaknesses, and so on. Then, each team member would get their marching orders. Which players to guard, which plays to run, and when.

After the scouting report, the dreaded Sustagen – a 1960s era energy drink – would come. We'd all have to finish it between 3 and 3:30 pm. There was no cheating. The team manager made sure of that. He would collect each can of the stuff to make sure we drank all of it. Players today must drink better-tasting stuff than that damn Sustagen.

Real food was our reward *after* games. Like me, the guys on the bench would be first to the locker room after the games were over. At home, ten buckets of Kentucky Fried Chicken would be waiting for us from a franchise owned by Chuck Schoenhofer. Knowing that chicken was waiting for us, we'd make a mad dash for that locker room.

After we showered and dressed, it was time for more food! At home games, the entire team was treated to a steak dinner at Brown's Grill, a famous restaurant in Wichita, right across the street from the largest hospital, Wesley, a little more than a mile from the Roundhouse. Mr. Brown, the owner who loved our team, would comp us all – the coaches, wives, the players.

We looked forward to those meals, especially the homemade lemon meringue pie for dessert.

\*\*\*

Apart from playing better players and in fuller arenas, travel was one of the biggest differences between playing on the freshman team and varsity—both in how we traveled and where we traveled.

As freshmen, we played junior college teams in Kansas. In 1963 Kansas roads were all two lanes. No lights. No passing lanes. No deer warning signs. Traveling to the games was not too bad in the daylight. However, after the games – in the dark, rain, sleet, snow, and fog – we had to return to Wichita no matter what. Some nights the bus driver could not see two feet out in front of the bus. On these occasions, I moved to the front seat. He needed a co-pilot. I was his man. I was so scared I had to watch with him.

We really moved on up when we got to varsity, though – from buses to airplanes. It was a world of difference.

The university contracted with Shamrock Airlines out of Oklahoma City to fly us all over the United States. The planes were converted into World War II-vintage DC 3s to transport parachute troops. Built in 1935, these planes were refurbished for public travel, seating between 30 and 40 passengers. With a top speed of just 180 MPH and a ceiling of 21,000 feet, we usually cruised at 16,000 ft. The maximum range was 1080 miles, or the exact distance between my hometown of Washington, Pennsylvania, and Wichita, Kansas.

You may be asking yourself: how do I know all this? Well, our pilot, Roxy Robertson, the brother of the cowboy movie star Dale Robertson, allowed us to visit with him in the cockpit doorway during the flights. He didn't just sit there. He explained all about the plane and its capabilities. Also, at 16,000 feet, what's on the ground is much more interesting than flying at today's altitude of 38,000 feet. I still remember when he pointed out the huge dome of clouds over St Louis a couple of hundred miles away.

One of the cool things about airplane travel is that we got to spend time with some real Wichita "fixtures" who traveled with us virtually everywhere we went. Jack Lynch, then the radio voice of the Shockers. Jack Miller, the sports director at the *Wichita Eagle* and liquor store owner at First and Indiana (I just wanted to sneak that latter part in!). Bill Hodges, the *Eagle's* sportswriter who covered our games. And Tommy Vickers, the owner of Vickers Oil, was a big supporter of the university and our team.

However, there were a few scary moments on our plane trips, which I won't forget. One was on a doubleheader road trip during the 1965-66 season. We played Southern Illinois on December 20$^{th}$ in Carbondale and the next day flew to Milwaukee to play Marquette on the 22$^{nd}$.

Sorry to say, but I remember a lot more about what happened on that flight we took out of Milwaukee right after the game than I do about both games themselves. We were all dead tired and sound asleep, helped by the sleep-inducing but nonetheless loud sound from those two prop engines.

And then sudden quiet. At 16,000 feet. It was enough to scare the "crap" out of everyone. Seriously. I really believed that the silence caused a few laundry problems that night.

The reason: Roxy comes over to the Com and says, "Sorry about that, fellas, we ran out of fuel, and we are on the spare tank. I am turning around and heading back to Lambert field to fill up." So, you do the math. This buggy has a maximum travel range of 1080 miles. Wichita to

Carbondale = 134 miles, Carbondale to Milwaukee = 421 miles, Milwaukee to Wichita = 762 miles. Total 1,183 miles one way from Wichita to Carbondale to Milwaukee and then back to Wichita (I didn't do all the precise math in my head then – there was no internet and there were no cell phones – but I had enough fear about how the math would work out!). Roxy tried to make it back to Wichita without refueling in Milwaukee. And 1,183 is greater than the plane's range of 1,080.

However, that is not the end of this wonderful adventure. Lambert field came over the Com: "DC3: your aircraft cannot land at Lambert; you have no radar for us to track you in. You must land at Midway. Midway has been shut down, but we will have someone go over there and turn on the runway lights for you." So, that's what the pilot did.

Thank goodness we landed safely. But we were all starving—no food on this buggy. The one assistant on our plane, the hero that night, got out her notepad and took hamburger orders. She walked over to a nearby hamburger bar so we would have something to eat.

We were still tired. At least we were not hungry anymore! Roxy filled her up, and off we flew. I can't vouch for the rest of the guys, but I could not close my eyes till I felt the wheels touch the ground in Wichita.

Tragically, the next airplane story I need to tell ended far worse. Two years after I graduated, the WSU Football Team was on a charter plane that crashed in Colorado on a trip to Utah in October of 1970. The pilots had plenty of warning about bad weather but had taken off in Denver, where the plane first stopped, anyhow. There is a memorial to all those who died on that trip at one of the entrances to the university off 17$^{th}$ street.

I never got on another plane – of any type – for ten years after that crash. In the early 1980's Nicky Cruz, author of *The Cross* and the *Switch Blade,* had a big gathering at East High School in Wichita. He was flying all over Europe, passing out Bibles in Russa. I walked backstage and visited with him. I told him of my fear of flying. He said, "Bob, there are a thousand ways you can die. You will not die in an airplane accident." I believed him. From that day forward, I flew everywhere, and it felt great to be flying again.

Fortunately, the scary airplane ventures for our basketball team were few and far between. The larger story about playing varsity is that we went to many different places. For kids growing up in small places, like I did, and like many of my teammates, varsity travel meant going to big cities, and seeing and experiencing things at an impressionable age many of us never would have imagined just a year before.

Dave Leach summed it up by describing to us his experience, which largely mirrored my own: "As a small-town kid from Kansas who had traveled across the Kansas line once before enrolling at the University of Wichita, the opportunity to see the 'outside world' was not only great fun but also a great education in and of itself. We traveled coast to coast and border to border during my playing years – New York, Philly, D.C., Chicago, Minneapolis, Denver, Dallas, El Paso, Phoenix, L.A., San Francisco, Salt Lake City, and Portland, among others. There was the thrill of playing in the 'old' Madison Square Garden and Chicago Stadium."

\*\*\*

I conclude this story of the ups and downs of being on a college basketball team in the 1960s with some words about a subject that still, unfortunately, is with us today in America. Racism.

We opened the book by discussing the limited opportunities great black athletes had to go to the colleges of their choice until all schools began accepting and recruiting them by the late 1960s and early 1970s. How did someone as great as Dave Stallworth, coming out of high school, had so few colleges from outside Texas, let alone inside the state, interested in him? Racism elsewhere, I am sad to say, is a major reason why Ralph Miller probably was able to persuade him to come to Wichita. Ralph also recruited a lot of other black athletes who helped put the Shockers on the national basketball map during his year coaching the team.

I will be the first to recognize the injustice of the discrimination that blacks faced in this country back when I was playing and still do today, though I believe there has been progress. But I can also honestly tell you that, from my vantage point, there was no racial tension on our team. On the contrary, we were all like family, black and white. It was real then and remains real amongst all of us who are still alive today.

But unfortunately, some fans in some places have not had the same attitude. One of those places was Tulsa, where our Shocker team has never been welcome, to put it mildly.

A distinct memory that I will always carry with me is how the bus we took from the airport to the Tulsa stadium had to be pulled up under the canopy of the rear entrance to the stadium, so close to the wall that no human body could reach in to harm us. After the game, the driver would ask us to put our heads down in crash position so any rocks that made it through the glass would not hit us in the head. We also never ate in any Tulsa restaurants for a similar reason.

Being from the small southwestern town in Pennsylvania, which everyone there referred to as a true melting pot, I could not for the life of me figure out where all this hate was coming from. In recent years, I learned the answer. In 1921, there were enough hateful residents in Tulsa that completely burned down the Greenwood section of town, known as "Black Wall Street". The dead were placed in mass graves without identification. It was one of the worst race riots in American history.

And until recently, not well known. My co-author Bob Litan, who grew up in Wichita, just 180 miles from Tulsa, was never taught about the Greenwood massacre in any of his middle or high school classes. I'll bet most Americans of that era had a similar experience.

I can't help but think that some of the same attitudes that led white Tulsans to commit such a massacre a long time were still held by some of those in the Tulsa stadium when we played. But we ignored it all and played together as a team, wherever we went.

The basketball court, at least for us, was a safe haven away from the racial injustice that we knew existed elsewhere in the country and even in our own city.

The Skys were not so friendly for the Shockers in the 60's

## Douglas DC-3

*The DC-3 was to become perhaps the most important airliner in history. It quickly established its reputation with many operators, including the military.*

"Our home away from home"

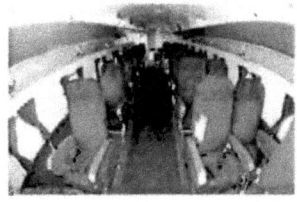

Action photos from the Parnassus yearbook

Brown's fed us after games

Kau Kau "Corner"

Middle row in the back, half of his face shown, is THE Chuck Schoenhofer, owner-operator. Far left in a suit is Hugh Stevens, Chuck's partner. On the far right were chefs. One was Alex Newhouse, the fullback Robert Newhouse's cousin, who played for the Dallas Cowboys. The other was a man named Al, last name unknown. I was born in 1960, so I have no idea if these people are still alive.

Courtesy of Mark T Schoenhofer, Son of Chuck Schoenhofer.

# Chapter Nine: The Knicks and Dave's Too Brief NBA Career

The NBA in the 1960s was nothing like it is today. The league had 18 teams, split between two divisions into two conferences. In contrast, to the 30 teams now, with three divisions per conference.

Nor was the NBA draft back then anything like the network television extravaganza today. In the 1960s, the draft was conducted by telephone out of the league office. Players, who were dispersed throughout the country either at home or on campuses, learned of their draft selections through their coaches via telephone calls or in-person meetings.

NBA draft day in 1965 was no different for Dave Stallworth than other days. He was about to play a pickup game on the Wichita State campus when he was told to come to the basketball office. There, he was phoned by the Knicks' front office to tell him he'd been selected as the third overall pick in the draft, behind Davidson's Fred Hetzel and Miami's Rick Barry. The Knicks also took Bill Bradley in a separate "regional" draft (those no longer exist).

The Cincinnati Royals also drafted Nate Bowman in the first round in 1965. He was moved to the Chicago Bulls the following season as part of the league's expansion draft but broke his leg and played limited minutes. The Knicks picked him up as a backup center in 1967, where he was reunited with Stallworth and stayed through the 1970 championship season.

\*\*\*

Dave joined a Knicks team that struggled the previous year with a 31-49 record, which was why the Knicks had the third pick in the draft. The team's center, Willis Reed, who later became famous during the Knicks' 1970 title season, was named the league's Rookie of the Year that year.

One of Reed's teammates was the number one overall pick in the draft the previous year, Jim "Bad News" Barnes of Texas Western. Barnes was well known to the Shockers, who played against him in college and was one of the team's toughest opposing players. So tough that Barnes was given the nickname by his teammates – "Bad News" – because of the havoc he would wreak on opposing teams.

New York traded Barnes to the Baltimore Bullets early the following year, despite his 16 points per game scoring average in his rookie year, for Walt Bellamy. Barnes eventually played on the 1968-69 Boston Celtic team that won the NBA championship that year. Remarking on his early death at age 63 due to heart problems, in a *Washington*

*Times* article in 2002, famed Celtic coach Red Auerbach called him a "great human being" – nothing like that nickname for which he was famous.

A major reason the Knicks had lopsided losing seasons is that they played in a tough four-team Eastern conference, dominated by the Boston Celtics and Philadelphia, with the Cincinnati Royals (and the Big "O") close behind. Dave's arrival in New York didn't immediately change the Knicks' fortunes. The Knicks were 30-50 his first year.

Still, Dave made major contributions as a $6^{th}$ or $7^{th}$ man, racking up almost 13 points per game with about 24 minutes of average playing time. A very good showing, but not enough to overcome the San Francisco Warriors' Rick Barry, with a scoring average of almost 26 points per game, for Rookie of the Year honors.

*\*\*\**

The Knicks' record improved slightly in the 1966-67 season, to 36-45, while Dave's numbers stayed about the same through March. But on March 7, 1967, in a game against the Warriors in Fresno, California, he would suffer the first major setback of his life, which would also prove to be life-changing.

As he was warming up, he took a left-handed hook shot. Then *slam*. Dave recounted to New York sportswriter Jay

Neugeboren in 1970 (whose account of the events that follow we draw on here): "I felt a knot in my chest, an uncomfortable feeling, kind of like someone was jumping up and down on my chest. I told Dick (McGuire, then the Knicks coach) that I didn't feel well." McGuire sat him out of the game.

He had no warning. That afternoon everything was normal. Dave and his teammates had been "laying around", watching TV. He had a ham sandwich and a coke for supper and then went to the arena.

As he explained to Neugeboren, it was "real hot" when they arrived. Several Knicks players asked the authorities to turn down the heat, which they did somewhat. But it was still hot.

Stallworth took off his sweats and began warming up. He said he felt okay. In his words: "I went to one end of the court and shot some jump shots – jump, jump, jump –Then I took this soft, easy hook shot, lefty, and...."

He initially thought it was indigestion, but the pain remained. The Warriors' doctor arranged for Dave to take an EKG the next day. It was negative, so he was cleared to play the next night in San Francisco, which he did. He felt fine then, too. If he hadn't been hit in the leg, he would have played more.

Two days later, when he returned to New York, Dave went to a heart specialist recommended by the team. He took another EKG, and this time it was positive. The docs immediately sent him to St. Clare's hospital, where more tests were run. The results: Dave had suffered a mild heart attack. According to the docs, it was a miracle he had played that second game in San Francisco and survived at all.

Hell followed. The docs ordered Dave to spend nearly a month on his back in the hospital. With no visitors. And no encouraging words from anyone. As he recalled it: "They tried to let me down easy. But what they were saying was that my career was over." At age 25. At close to the beginning of his NBA career. As Dave told the *Dallas Morning News* years later, "That's where [the hospital stay] I lost it. I didn't have any stamina after that."

But Dave is a fighter with an optimistic spirit. Always was before he came to Wichita, while he played for the Shockers and the Knicks. So picked himself off the proverbial mat and returned to Wichita, taking 12 more hours of coursework at the university, and slowly began to exercise.

Gradually, his health improved. He played golf (remember his golf talent we discussed earlier!). He went for regular medical exams. Did some scouting for the Knicks.

And as he felt better, he began playing pickup basketball without telling his doctors.

As Dave told Neugeboren, "I'd be sure never to play on a day when I had a doctor's visit, you know? I'd sneak in as much as possible – going slow at first, then faster when nothing bad happened. The guys in the schoolyard, I think they were more scared than I was. They treated me like an invalid. They'd throw a basketball and tell me to shoot baskets by myself while they played halfcourt. They razzed me. Carl Williams, one of my closest friends, he'd say: There comes the man with no heart."

In his second year after the (apparent) attack, Dave coached the Wichita Builders of the National Amateur Basketball Association to an undefeated 28-0 season. The team made it to the national finals, only to lose by one point to Tacoma, Washington.

Dave never got used to the idea that 'I could never play again." He poignantly added to Neugeboren: "I mean, basketball was my whole life. You know?"

And then his luck turned. In early 1969, or about 8-9 months before the 1969-70 season would begin, his docs told him he was cleared to play again. Dave "felt like he could jump over a building" hearing this news. Immediately calling the Knicks, he was told to return to New York. After passing the medical checkups, the Knicks gave him a new contract.

According to the *Dallas Morning News*, the contract was late in coming. Dave and his docs were convinced the year before that, in fact, he had never suffered a heart attack. But the Knicks and the NBA, fearing a relapse or a possible liability lawsuit, wanted to wait until the 1969-70 season to have Dave back.

Once he rejoined the Knicks, Dave gradually worked his way back into shape during 10 exhibition games. He averaged 10 points per game, establishing his role as at least a reserve forward going into the regular season.

On October 4, 1969, more than 2 and a half years since his hospitalization, Dave returned to Madison Square Garden as the seasoned opened with the Knicks facing the Seattle Supersonics. The *New York Daily News* had this account of what happened before the game began.

The Knicks' legendary John Condon (we can still hear his deep, resonant voice in our heads from watching Knick games on TV) started introducing the Knicks' players. When Condon got to Stallworth, he simply said: "Number 9... Dave Stallworth." The Garden "exploded".

The nearly 15,000 fans in the stands didn't just give him a standing ovation. According to the *New York Daily News*, the "Garden was rocking to the rafters with their cheers, shouts, and applause."

As all this mayhem was unfolding, Dave just bowed his head while his teammates, according to Jay Neugeboren's account the following year, "wore grins that were almost as broad as the one Dave would wear after the game." Why wouldn't they? The *Daily News* account says it all: "They [the fans and Dave's teammates] were witnesses to the greatest comeback in the history of professional sports."

\*\*\*

We got goosebumps just reading this account and writing it above. The game itself played out as if in a dream. Dave was the first Knicks sub inserted into the game in the first half and understandably a bit "tight". He got that out of his system in the second half. We'll let Neugeboren's account of what happened to speak for itself:

"In the second half, [Dave] hit on three beautiful jump shots, stole the ball three times, picked off six rebounds, went through the longest gasp of the night on a gorgeous left-side drive where he suddenly stopped, and – his body still moving toward the basket, the defender caught flat-footed – he swished in a wide, easy left-handed hook shot." The same shot he took when those chest pains first hit him and almost ended his career.

The Knicks easily won that opening game by 25 points. They would go on to have a historic regular season, with a 60-22 record. Much of the team's turnaround can be attributed to their (now) Hall of Fame coach, Red Holzman, who was hired in 1968 to replace Dick McGuire. Red was fortunate, of course, to have five starters willing to play the "team first" basketball, the style he wanted. All starters still scored in double digits: Willis Reed, Walt ("Clyde") Frazier, Bill Bradley, Dave DeBusschere, and Dick Barnett. With Stallworth's college rival, Cazzie Russell, coming off the bench as the 6th man.

Dave contributed to the team's success but didn't get the minutes he had before his scary episode: averaging almost 17 per game versus 24 before. His scoring average dipped below 8 points per game versus about 13 before. He did play in all 82 regular-season games.

His Wichita State teammate, Nate Bowman, who had been traded to the Knicks, also played in almost every regular season game as Willis Reed's backup, averaging 9 minutes, 3 points, and 3 rebounds per game.

But it wasn't the regular season for which Dave long will be remembered, along with his comeback on that incredible opening night of the season.

It was the fifth game of the NBA finals in 1970 against the Los Angeles Lakers, a team that had also finished first in its conference. The Lakers were led by NBA legends Wilt Chamberlin and Jerry West. They had barely lost out on winning the championship the previous year to the Celtics in a classic 7th game, and were clearly hungry to finally win a title without having to face the Celtics in the final series.

Going into the 5th game of the series, on May 4, 1970, at the Garden, the two teams were even, having split the first four games. Eight minutes into that 5th game, the Knicks' center, Willis Reed, seriously injured his right hip and had to leave the game, with his team trailing by 10. By halftime, the Knicks were down 13, and things looked bleak.

The Knicks had put their backup center Nate Bowman in to try to slow Chamberlin down in the first half, but it wasn't working. All Red Holzman could do was gamble. But what gamble? At halftime, Bill Bradley suggested that the Knicks try a 1-3-1 zone defense, with three guards or wingman in the middle to disrupt West's passing into Chamberlin. One under-sized Knick would hang back with Chamberlin, hoping for some help from the middle of the defense to collapse when the ball went to Wilt.

It was a college defense for a pro game against one of the most dominant centers in NBA history. Holzman took

Bradley's suggestion (he was a Rhode scholar, how could you question him?) So, opening the second half, the Knicks used DeBusschere against Chamberlin, but DeBusschere eventually got into foul trouble. Red then asked Stallworth, "Can you handle him?" Dave answered, "We'll find a way." At 6' 7" up against the 7' 1" Lakers' giant.

Didn't he? Stallworth outscored Wilt 10-0 over the game's last nine minutes. Near the end of the game, Dave drove to the basket against Chamberlin and put in a picture-perfect reverse layup. Wayne Coffey of the *New York Daily News* called it "one of the single most dramatic moments of the season".

Over the entire second half, DeBusschere and Stallworth held Wilt to just four points. The Knicks' swarming defense up front in that zone helped, denying the ball to Chamberlin. But when the ball got to Wilt, the two Dave's were there, too.

As Stallworth recounted to the *Dallas Morning News* years later, "Every time he [Wilt] put it on the floor, I would steal it from him. I think I caught him by surprise more than anything."

The whole Lakers were surprised. So much so that they lost 107-100, with the Knicks mounting a 20-point swing, using an undersized 1-3-1 defense to pull off the miracle.

***

Wilt and the Lakers got their revenge for the next game in Los Angeles and played without Reed. Wilt scored 45, many on virtually on uncontested dunks.

The deciding 7$^{th}$ game returned to the Garden. No one knew if Reed was well enough to play. But he came out to warm up about an hour before the game began and hit a few shots before returning to the clubhouse. Chamberlin and West looked on, wondering whether Reed would return for the game itself like everyone else. When the Knicks' starting lineup was introduced later, and John Condon pronounced those magic words "Captain Willis Reed", the Garden exploded.

Although Reed was hobbled during the game, he scored the first two baskets, though no more than the rest of the way. He didn't have to. His mere presence inspired the rest of the team to greatness. They went on a tear, leading at one point in the first half by 29 points. The Knicks easily won the game – and the championship – with Clyde Frazier playing the game of his life, with 36 points, 19 assists, and 7 rebounds. It helped that Red Holzman kept Frazier off Jerry West on defense, which kept Frazier from getting into foul trouble. The final score was 113-99.

Nate Bowman played a solid 21 minutes in that 7th and deciding game, spelling the hobbled Reed. Nate logged 6 points and 5 rebounds. (Little known fact: Nate Bowman gave Clyde his famous nickname because his tailored suits made him look like "Clyde" of Bonnie and Clyde).

That 7th game has since been known as the "Willis Reed game". Just say those words, and every NBA fan knows what you're talking about.

But what most fans don't know is that there would never have been a Willis Reed game if Dave Stallworth had not saved the Knicks in that crucial game 5 with a legendary performance of his own. As fellow Knick "Minute Man" (as the Knick reserves were called), Mike Riordan recounted to the *New York Post:* "We didn't have any right winning that game. To me, that was the key game."

Yes, Mike, to you and every other knowledgeable fan. *That* was the key game to the series and the Knicks' ultimate triumph.

***

Dave played more the following year with the Knicks, averaging nearly 20 minutes and 10 points per game. But early in the 1971-72 season, he was traded – there is little loyalty in professional sports, which is a business first and foremost – along with Knick reserve Mike Riordan to the

Baltimore Bullets for Earl ("the Pearl") Monroe, who at the time was in a bitter money dispute with the Bullets. With Monroe, the Knicks would win the NBA title in 1973, beating the Lakers 4-1.

Stallworth, meanwhile, got even more playing time in Baltimore for the first year he was there, 28 minutes per game, enough time to put in an average of 11 points and pull down 6 rebounds per game. After Dave's first year with the team, he was used more sparingly in the following two years (The Bullets moved to Washington and became the Capital Bullets in 1973). In 1974, the Bullets traded him to Phoenix, which promptly sent Dave back to Knicks to close his career. After playing in 7 games that 1974-75 season, Dave retired.

For his entire NBA career, which spanned 6 seasons of playing time, Dave averaged 20 minutes, 9 points, and 5 rebounds per game.

There is no question that Dave's heart issue – and the fears by the Knicks and other teams that might have taken him on instead – kept him from being a starter and having a longer and more prolific career. Had the same thing that happened to Dave on that fateful day in March 1967 happened today, with all the advances in medical science since doctors would have discovered sooner that Dave probably never did have a heart attack. And had that happened, Dave's value to the Knicks or other teams surely would have been greater than it was. He would have gotten more playing time to prove to the NBA that he was as good as he was in college and touted to be coming into the NBA.

According to all the public reporting we have reviewed, Dave, remarkably, was never bitter about all this, at least openly. He took it all in stride and, like all of us who have had misfortunes in life, just put one foot in front of the other – each day, as readers will learn in the next chapter.

Dave's teammate, Nate Bowman, had it worse. The Knicks traded him to Buffalo after their 1970 championship season. Nate played in the ABA with Pittsburgh one more year before retiring in 1972. After basketball, he became a personal bodyguard. In an ironic and sad twist, given what had most thought had happened to Stallworth, Bowman died of a heart attack in 1984, right after auditioning for a Miller beer television commercial in mid-town New York.

## Chapter Ten: Life after Basketball

As hard as it is to believe today – when even NBA reserves, after free agency kicks in, can command annual salaries in the $10 million range – Dave Stallworth earned just $55,000 at his peak. He started at $11,000.

Dave wasn't alone in being paid a pittance for his talents. NBA legends Wilt Chamberlin and Bill Russell didn't hit the $100,000 salary mark until 1965.

The major reason that NBA salaries are as high as they are today – with superstars making $40 million a year or more – dates to a pathbreaking event in 1976, the year after Dave retired, for which one of Dave's NBA opponents was largely responsible.

That event was *free agency,* which means that after the first couple of years in the league, players (mostly through their agents) can shop around among teams (employers) for the best deal, just like other workers in our economy.

Free agency didn't just happen. As in other professional sports, the NBA agreed to it because it had been sued under the antitrust laws for unlawfully conspiring to limit player salaries by binding players to their teams unless the teams no longer wanted their services (the infamous "reserve" clause).

The plaintiff was none other than NBA legend Oscar Robertson, who wanted on behalf of all NBA players a lot more than free agency, including the end of the college draft. The parties settled instead on free agency for the current and future players.

Free agency did what one would have expected in a free market for superior basketball talent. It led to much higher salaries, which grew over time as the NBA became more popular and brought in more money. Money that, by virtue of a labor agreement with the NBA players' union, NBA teams essentially shared with the players, up to a point. At the behest of the teams, the players accepted-salary caps for entire teams and superstar players.

Had Dave Stallworth been able to play a few more years into free agency, which might have happened had he had more modern medical care when he had those chest pains on that night in March of 1976, he would have been able to leave basketball with at least some money in the bank to carry him through the next phase of his life.

Was he ever bitter about the fact that he didn't, especially as he grew older, watching NBA games on TV? Knowing what the other players were making, most of them with lesser skills than him. And what he could have made?

In our interviews and researching the public record, there is no evidence of any bitterness. Just a matter-of-fact acceptance of that's the way things were. And that he felt himself lucky to have played in the NBA at all.

*** 

Given his financial circumstances, Dave needed a job or to open a business to make ends meet for himself and his family. He first tried his hand at launching a business, figuring that his best chances of succeeding were in Wichita, where he was a household name.

His first and apparently only attempt to strike out on his own was a plan to open a gym (what today would be called a "health club") at 21st and Oliver, not far from the Wichita State campus. At the time, it was a far safer neighborhood than it has become. He tried to get bank backing for the project, but it never came through. We have no idea whether Dave approached Wichita State basketball backers for some equity funding, but given his fame, one would have thought he and his idea would have been accepted with open arms.

Whatever the reason, and it is possible to suspect the worst (that he was black), Dave's gym plans never panned out. For a time after that, he worked at a recreation center at 17$^{th}$ and Hillside, right on the corner of the Wichita State campus.

In 1978, Dave found a better job at Wichita's largest employer, Boeing. Its plant in southern Wichita was more like its own city; it was that large. With huge buildings where jetliners were built. With runways to fly planes in and out. Close to McConnell air force base, with its own city-like presence.

Dave's job was to distribute parts to the various stations within the manufacturing behemoth. There he would stay until 2005 after Boeing was sold to Spirit and the new company had no place for him.

In what is a vast understatement, working as a parts distributor alongside other plant workers and reporting to managers who oversaw the whole process was a long way from playing basketball at the highest level, in arenas with 15,000 or more fans screaming. On national TV, when the playoffs came around.

But by all accounts, Dave took it in stride. He never showed unhappiness about his new life, the one he would live out the rest of his working years.

Without explicitly acknowledging these words, Dave had to experience what all athletes eventually must face. That "retiring" from competitive sports is like a first death. It takes away, at least temporarily, your identity or even reason for being.

In the words of Bishop Ronald Gilmore, who has helped Bob Powers' through much of his life, describing the challenges of his (Gilmore's) own retirement:

"But then you retire, and that wind is gone. Suddenly "gone". Today an unsettling storm; tomorrow, an unsettling stillness. You get so used to leaning into that wind, and you damn-near fall over when that wind is no longer there." [From Gilmore, *The Uncommandments of Growing Old.*].

Surely, Dave must have felt, even if fleetingly, that he would "damn-near fall over" too after basketball. But if he did, he never outwardly showed it.

\*\*\*

There was one especially bright spot in Dave's return to Wichita, however, that would prove invaluable for the rest of his life.

By returning to his college "home" and working at Boeing, Dave met Gloria Jones in 1982, who not only also worked at Boeing but lived in the same Cherry Hill apartment building near Boeing and McConnell as Dave did.

Dave always had a very private life, which he kept to himself, even when talking to reporters. So, we do not know how and when it happened (nor did we want to pry out of respect to Dave), but Dave and Judy divorced. Dave also was divorced from a second wife.

Dave had and was raising three children before he met Gloria. Dana Lyn is now living in Las Vegas with three children of her own. Lenita works in hotel management in the San Francisco area. Paul David, who played organized basketball and tennis at Southeast high school (and attended a basketball camp run by Dave's Knick teammate Willis Reed), is living in California.

Gloria had two children of her own when she met Dave, Ailah (today a cosmetologist working in Wichita), and Hameed (who works today for Cargill, also in Wichita). After high school (where, in the small world department, she was in the same graduating class as Bob Litan), Gloria initially attended El Reno junior college and later Wichita State, intending to get her degree to become a pharmacist. For a time, Gloria worked in the pharmacy department of Wesley Medical Center, the largest healthcare facility in the Wichita area. Eventually, however, Gloria found her way to Boeing, which helped finance the completion of her B.S. and Masters' degrees in human resources at Friends University, a small well-regarded college in Wichita.

Dave met Gloria when he was nearing 40. The two of them hit off, dated for three years, and then were married.

As quiet, private people, they were clearly meant for each other. Dave was humble and easygoing. Gloria was beautiful and elegant, with determination honed by experience.

After marriage, Dave and Gloria moved to more central Wichita locations. They lived a quiet middle-class life, working during the day and socializing on some nights and weekends with a close group of other couples.

They also did what other people did. They always went to church. Every Saturday, they went to Jimmie's, a famous breakfast place in Wichita. They took nice vacations when they had the chance—one memorable cruise to the Bahamas. But without any fanfare, one would associate with a former basketball star.

Dave & Gloria 1987

Not a special occasion, just a photo for themselves

Dave & Gloria Stallworth ate at Jimmies many Sundays after church

Jack, Linda & Joey Davidson of Jimmie's

Thank you, Wichita

Indeed, Gloria told us that Dave rarely talked about his basketball life. Been there, done that.

It was not a perfect life – whose is? But one of the obstacles both had to face was not of their own making. Readers will guess what that obstacle was, of course. It was racial discrimination.

Gloria had it the toughest. At Boeing, Gloria worked in inspection. One of the few women to do so. Moreover,

Gloria was a black woman in a plant where only whites, especially white men, worked.

Trouble in this environment was inevitable, though perhaps only in retrospect. One day at work, Gloria returned to her work area to find a hangman's noose lying there. She reported the incident to the HR department at Boeing, after which she was closely watched by her supervisor, clearly looking for any "mistake" or excuse to fire her.

Gloria's complaint led to an internal hearing, for which she received no notice. At the time, she didn't know it would have helped to have hired a lawyer. In the end, though, things worked out. "Some good white people" stood up for and assisted her. Eventually, her supervisor and another individual were fired.

As a Wichita basketball icon, it was a lot easier for Dave. But he, too, nonetheless could not change the color of his skin or the racial attitudes of some of his co-workers. He suffered racial slights at various points in his Boeing career, too. Unfortunately, with all his fame in the city where he became famous, even Dave Stallworth could not totally escape racism.

***

Dave didn't give up basketball entirely. He had several opportunities to offer basketball commentary as a guest on

Mike Kennedy's broadcasts of Wichita State's basketball games. Kennedy told us that Dave provided insights that only a former pro player could provide when he appeared. Like knowing player tendencies, whether they tended to favor going left or right. And how to guard them.

Dave also became a fixture at Wichita State home games, where he had lifetime season tickets. Always willing to sign autographs. Flashed that trademark smile.

We were fortunate to see Dave, with all his teammates, brought together in March 2015, on the 50th anniversary of the Shocker's going to the Final Four. One of us (Powers) was the organizer, and the other (Litan) was a lucky attendee.

Powers knew well before that night that the 50th anniversary was upcoming the following year. And that it could very well be the last time that all remaining players from that team could be together (several had already passed on to "Sky Hoops", as Powers calls it). So, any anniversary event just had to be a big deal.

Powers ensured that it was. Making sure the *Eagle* would write about it (which is how Litan made sure he and three guests would come, a night that would lead to the authors' close friendship and the events described in the concluding chapter). Calling major supporters of Shocker basketball to ensure they bought tickets and arranging all the event details.

The event was a magical night – a dinner and speech event held at Wichita's Broadview Hotel. After a cocktail hour that allowed the players to be reunited with each other and dinner, the main events began.

They opened with an emotional tribute to someone who wasn't even on the team, Powers' high school basketball teammate Marine Private First Class John Daniel Slesh. Although limited in athletic ability, John was the hardest worker on Powers' team. After graduation, Slesh enlisted in the Marine Corps when the Vietnam War was in its initial stages.

The Marine Corps' honor guard played taps at the beginning of the ceremony to honor John's immense bravery and sacrifice in Vietnam. You see, John threw his body on a live grenade to save the life of his superior officer. The place was so silent you could hear a pin drop while John's story was retold. God bless you, John Slesh.

It was difficult after that tribute to go on. But Masters of Ceremonies, Mike Kennedy and his broadcast partner Dave Dahl, another former Shocker player, did so with aplomb. They introduced each of the players, coaches, and managers, including the too many of them who had since passed on. The introductions included a brief history of how each came to Wichita and the contributions each made to the 1964-65 team. In writing this book, the two of us drew on those intros, together with some memorable anecdotes told by the players at a breakfast the following morning.

Then Wichita State head basketball coach Gregg Marshall – who had coached the Shockers to their only other Final Four appearance in 2013 – gave a 45-minute stemwinder about his life in basketball and what the sport meant to all of those there and the entire Shocker fan base. It was a tour de force, one of the greatest speeches many of us had ever heard.

All the surviving members of the 1964-65 team, most with their spouses and families, were there. But there was no question that Dave Stallworth's presence was the real main event. Everyone there knew that even though Dave couldn't be with the team during its second half of the season Cinderella run to the Final Four, he was the reason they were in a position even to make that run. He was the inspiration that drove the entire team to perform the magic that got them there. The standing ovation Dave received upon being formally introduced was lengthy and loud.

By then, however, Dave was in a wheelchair. Starting around 2004, the year before he retired, Dave began to have real heart problems.

But to everyone who approached Dave just to talk, to thank him for all he did for the University and Wichita, and for all that he meant to their lives – your authors included – Dave could not have been nicer. Or humbler. And always with that smile.

***

After that memorable reunion, Dave's failing health continued its inevitable decline. After the 50<sup>th</sup> event, Powers made several visits to Dave's house. From here to the rest chapter, we switch back to Bob in the first person.

When I got to the house, I would go out to North Wichita, where he lived, about 5 miles from my house. I would knock on the door, and Gloria would let me in. I'd go to the living room where Dave would be playing with his grandson. He and I would visit a little then I would be on my way.

A month or two later, I showed up again. Gloria led me to the living room while she went to get Dave. He would come out of his bedroom with his walker. We sat and visited a bit.

Another month or so later, when I got to the house, Gloria led me directly back to his bedroom, where Dave was in his chair watching TV.

Several weeks later, Gloria simply said for me to go on back to his room myself. She warned Dave was in his bed, but "you can see him". The TV was off, and Dave was in and out of consciousness under his covers.

That was the last time I saw Dave alive. It was clear to the very end that Dave was a true "ROUNDBALLER". Gloria had his Chuck Taylors on him laced up and ready for his first "Sky Hoops" game. March 16, 2017.

John Daniel Slesh

Private First Class

F CO, 2ND BN, 9TH MARINES, 3RD MARDIV, III MAF

United States Marine Corps

Washington, Pennsylvania

March 14, 1946, to May 08, 1967

JOHN D SLESH is on the Wall at Panel 19E, Line 66

See the full profile or name rubbing for John Slesh

50th Reunion Game Night

Introducing Dave 'The Rave" Stallworth

Tommy & Bob telling Dave the Shocker crowd is giving him another standing "Ovation"

50th Reunion February 6th, 2015 Missouri State vs. Wichita State Halftime

Front Row:

Manny Zafiros, Tommy Newman, Wheel Chair David Stallworth, Mohamed Sharif, Johnny Criss, Diane Coons, Dee Heller, Dee Anderson, Don Harmison, Betty Thomson, Chuck Brosky, Lanny VanEman, WU Shock.

Back Row:

David Nelson, David Leach, Al Trope, Bob Powers, Melvin Reed, Gerald Davis, Vern Smith, Jerry Reimond, Larry Nosich

# Chapter Eleven: Honoring Dave Forever

After the shock and sadness of Dave's passing, I couldn't sit still (this is Bob Powers again talking in the first person). I just had to do something to ensure that Dave would never be forgotten. Melvin Reed and Mohamed Sharif felt the same way.

Ideas flew. What about naming a street after him? A bridge? After a few days, I settled on something different.

A statue of Dave to remind everyone of his greatness (there were no other statues of basketball players anywhere in Wichita at the time). And ideally, a scholarship fund at Wichita State was named after him to help worthy students – later to be determined to be students majoring in education.

I ran the idea by several of my teammates and multiple Wichita notables, all of whom agreed it was the right thing to do. The challenges then were three-fold. Find someone to design the statue. Decide where it would go. Raise the money to make it happen!

This project brought me together with my now close friend Bob Litan, who was smitten by Dave from the time he was ten years old when Dave first joined the Shockers. That admiration and loyalty literally was hard-wired into Bob's heart and soul that February 1963 night when Bob was able to witness Dave's 46 point legendary performance upsetting, then number one ranked Cincinnati from ground floor seats. Bob never forgot that night or what Dave Stallworth meant to him growing up and to Wichita, memories which led him to join forces with the other Bob (Powers) to raise money for the statue and the scholarship fund and to plan the ceremonies when the project was completed.

*** 

What pose should the statute take, and who should sculpt it? My initial thought was to approach the Wichita State art department. But I wanted a wider scan before making any final decision. So, I put out the word, and soon my texts, emails, and the phone began lighting up.

A timely call from Dave Leach, our team captain, put all the uncertainty to rest. Dave highly recommended a close friend, Ann LaRose, a nationally recognized sculptor. After contacting her and discussing some general ideas for the statue, she came up with the perfect design, the one readers see on the cover. It was Dave's classic pose, "Our All American", shooting his famous jump shot.

Ann has had numerous sculpting commissions in the United States and throughout the world. Much of her childhood was spent in Europe, where she was greatly impressed by the realistic bronze sculpture created there for centuries. On a trip to Italy at age fifteen, Ann decided that she wanted to be a sculptor, but it wasn't until a trip to Art Castings of Colorado in 1979 that she realized her goal was possible. Ann's college arts degree, which she received in 1970, is from the Oklahoma College of Liberal Arts. I can safely say that everyone in the Wichita community is grateful to Ann and her husband and business partner, Bruce, for creating Dave's magnificent statue.

Our next challenge was to figure out where the statue should be located. My initial thought was to have it placed in the lobby of Charles Koch Arena, the renovated and renamed stadium where Dave played his home games. With the help of then Wichita State president John Bardo (who tragically died of lung disease in March 2019, almost two years to the day after Dave passed), and then Wichita State athletic director Darron Boatwright, we decided instead to place the statue, where it sits today. We hope forever: IN FRONT of Koch Arena so that everyone who comes into the arena will be reminded of the once-in-a-generation talents of the gentle and humble man who put Wichita State basketball on the national map.

Finally, we had to raise money, not just for the statue, but for a scholarship fund at the university bearing Dave's name. To be honest, some at the outset questioned whether we could do it. But I knew from having lived in Wichita since I graduated that there were plenty of people who felt like Bob Litan and I did about Dave and would help financially. Some of those were members of the fund-raising committee we put together and who we cannot thank enough for coming through in a big way: Gerry Aaron, Gary Austerman, Cindy Carnahan, Tom Devlin (for whom the basketball court in Koch arena is named), and Herb Krumsick (a member of Wichita State's 1963 football team that won the Missouri Valley Conference championship and who knew Dave while they were in college). We couldn't have pulled it off without great help from Wichita State's athletic organization and foundation.

Dave's statue was unveiled on December 5, 2018. It was an overcast day, but the ceremony held right before it was memorable, as was the dinner the night before, when one more time, many of Dave's teammates joined together to celebrate his life. In the same room at the Broadview Hotel where the 50$^{th}$-anniversary dinner had been held about three and a half years before.

Thanks to the generosity of all those who contributed, we were able to complete the statue's funding and still had some money left over for the scholarship fund. But we're not done.

The scholarship fund, and the future students who will benefit from it, still need more resources. We hope that this inspirational story of Dave Stallworth will help achieve that goal while ensuring that his legacy will never be forgotten.

Mike Kennedy

The Maestro himself as Co-Host at the David Stallworth Memorial dinner 2017

Memorial Dinner

Charlotte Scott, Dave's sister Lenita Stallworth, Dave's daughter

Dedication Dinner for the David Stallworth Memorial Statue

Kara Johnson WSU Foundation Robert Litan MC

Ann La Rose Sculptor

Herb Krumsick presents to the David Stallworth Memorial Dinner guests in 2018

1963 Shocker Football Team, MVC Champions

Herb Krumsick, Second Row 5th from right.

Lifetime Kansan. His Shocker "SUPPORT" over the years has been "UNQUESTIONABLE" and "INVALUABLE"

Darron & Kim Boatright Mike Kennedy John Dreifort

Enjoying the Reunion

Far left back Dwala Smith Bob Powers Gerry Reimond Marsha Allen, Rob Powers, and Dave Dahl working the room

Memorial Dinner

The Four Freshman

Al Trope, Bob Powers Melvin Reed Tommy Newman

Should be Five

Jamie Thompson went on to Sky Hoops in 2006 at the age of 61

We entered as Freshman together in August 1963

We have stayed together all these years

Memorial Dinner

Robert Litan Gloria Stallworth Melvin Reed Mohamed Sharif

Melvin presenting Gloria with a framed copy of the David Stallworth Memorial Scholarship

Statue Dedication

Dr. Chuck and Judy Brodsky

Team Manager taking a Break

JoAnn Powers and Bucky Walters

I told JoAnn to stay away from that Walters guy. He can be trouble

Lincoln Trower Dave Thomas

Thomas is the author of "JABALI" the book

(About Warren Armstrong Jabali)

John Dreifort Cleo Littleton

Cleo Littleton University of Wichita 1954 All-American

We are always "HONORED" by your presence Cleo

At every reunion event, a table and place setting was reserved for each of our 64-65 Final Four team members who have moved on to "Sky Hoops"

David Stallworth G, C, F 2017 age 75

Gary Thompson Head Coach 2010 age 78

Jamie Thompson Forward 2006 age 61

Ron Heller Asst Coach 2006 age 68

Verlyn Anderson Asst Coach 1994 age 60

Nate Bowman Center 1984 Age 41

Tom Reeves Head Trainer 1970 Age 30

Sculptor Ann LaRose in her office

Mohamed, " I think she has it right."

Mohamed & Bob meet in Boulder, Colorado

Final sign-off before Dave is bronzed

Ann LaRose Sculptor center gold shirt with her team taking a break for this photo

Marsha and Bob Allen watch party at Statue Dedication Day

From left: Bob Powers, JoAnn Powers, Mary Lou Smith, Jim Smith, Margo McDonald, Dave McDonald, Gloria Stallworth, Greg Bucchin, Kathy Bucchin, Bob Allen, Dee Williams, Martha Allen

Statue Dedication Day

Gloria Stallworth at center

**Statue Dedication**

**Hameed Holt,** Gloria's son **Gloria K'Mari Holt** Gloria's grandson

Gloria's baby grandson

**"King Holt"**

Kenney Lee and Gloria

Kenney was Dave's close friend from their 1960's football & basketball days

Unveiling Dave's Statue Gloria's first expression
**Qyree Holt** Gloria's grandson **Gloria K 'mari Holt**
Gloria's grandson
**Hameed Holt,** Gloria's son wearing Dave's Knicks 1970 World Championship Jacket

Statue looking west

The gang's all here

From left

Herb Krumsick, Darron Boatright, Cindi Carnahan, Tom Devlin

Gary Austerman, Bob Powers, Nick Jimenez ,Ralph Jimenez, Robert Litan, Jerry Aaron

Looking proud

Ann LaRose

Sculptor

Melvin Reed #20

My great and life long friend

Gerry Davis #10 Gerry

Quiet man about campus

Tommy #24 and Dianne Newman

High school sweethearts

JoAnn and I have been very special friends with Tommy & Dianne for the past 55 years

The 1964-65 Final Four team in the flesh

(With some honorary members)

Lean Mean Fighting Machines

From left back

David, Chuck, Tommy, Vern, Melvin, Al, Lanny, Gerry D., Dave, Mohamed, Johnny

From left bottom

Jamies Thompson's grandson, James Savage Nelson, Manny, Jerry R., Bob P., Gloria, Bob L.

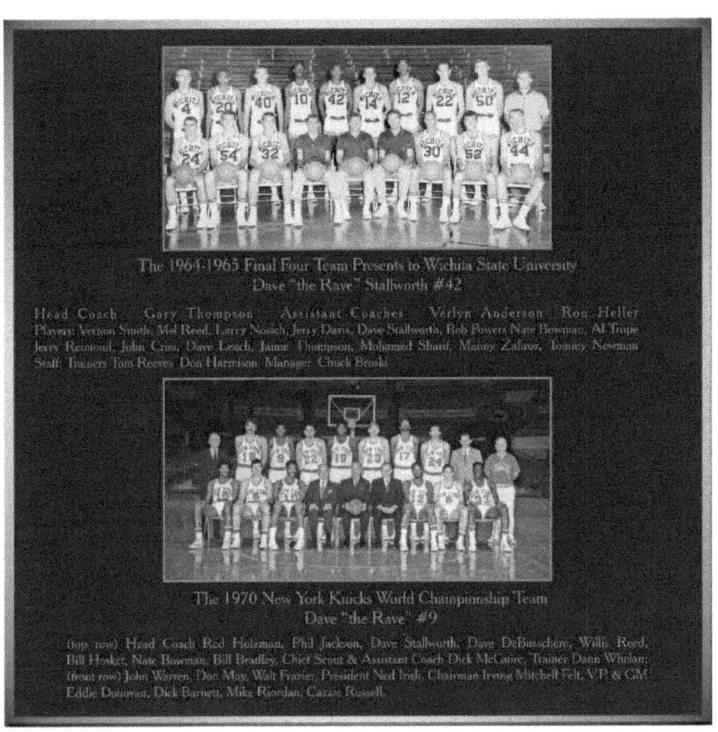

East bronze plaque on the base of statue

## Dave "The Rave" Stallworth
### December 20, 1941 - March 15, 2017

Born December 20, 1941 in Dallas, Texas. His mother, Doris, raised him in the housing projects of South Oak Cliff. While his grade school, N.W. Harllee, had no gym, he learned to play basketball on the outdoor courts, and by high school, Dave took James Madison to the Texas State Championship in 1960. Having graduated midterm in 1961, he was recruited by Ralph Miller and enrolled at the University of Wichita.

Soon, this talented and exciting athlete began packing Charles Koch Arena, known then as the Henry Levitt Arena. As a 1964 consensus first team All-American, Dave averaged 24.2 points and 10.5 rebounds over his three-year collegiate career, totaled 1,936 points, and helped lead the Shockers to become a national powerhouse. Dave's jersey No. 42 was retired in 1974 never to be worn by another Shocker player.

Drafted as the third overall pick in the 1965 NBA Draft by the New York Knickerbockers, Dave played eight professional seasons in the National Basketball Association for the Knicks and Baltimore Bullets. He was a key member of the famed 1970 World Championship Team in New York.

After professional basketball, Dave returned to Wichita - the city that he loved - where he lived with his wife Gloria, working 25 years at the Boeing Company. Dave has five children: Dana, Lanita, Paul and two step children; Aylah and Hameed.

Dave will forever be remembered for his gentle and kind nature, especially his trademark smile. Wichita will always be proud of Dave "the Rave" Stallworth.

Bronze plaque on the base of the statue

Facing west

Daves "Chuck Taylors"

The base of the statue

Ready for "Sky Hoops"

The statue at night facing west

# Epilogue

After reading this book, you may get the impression that Bob Powers thinks he was the big cheese on the Wichita State basketball team. Let's set the record straight. He was anything but, as readers have learned by now.

But I (Powers speaking) am the last living player from the 1964-65 team alive in Wichita. I have worked throughout my life to help others. This book is one of those efforts.

I have joined together with my partner Bob Litan to write this book not only to remember Dave but to honor all his (and my) teammates. Each of us came to Wichita State from different backgrounds. Not one of us came from a wealthy family. Our families each have their own individual issues, as all families do.

But we all had one thing in common. We were teammates on a memorable team with one hugely memorable player, Dave "The Rave" Stallworth. It was an honor and privilege to play with him and to call him our friend.

Before the 1964-65 NCAA Final Four team all move on to sky hoops, the team is committed to growing the existing WSU David Stallworth Memorial Scholarship to cover the full year of tuition and expenses in memory of All-American "Dave the Rave" Stallworth. The WSU David Stallworth Scholarship originated as a way to honor David Stallworth and his legacy and was created by Robert Powers, Robert Litan, Gary Austerman, and Jerry Aaron. Just as the Shocker basketball program was forever changed by Dave Stallworth's humble and unselfish attitude, his supporters hope to continue this legacy by supporting bright students for generations to come.

With your help, this legacy will continue to grow. Please consider helping with a gift. Ways to give include visiting the Wichita State University Foundation website at:

www.foundation.wichita.edu or by mailing a check payable to:

WSU Foundation WSU David Stallworth Memorial Scholarship

1845 Fairmount Street

Wichita, KS 67260-0002

For the team

Bob Powers Teammate #14

## Stallworth Scholarship Meter

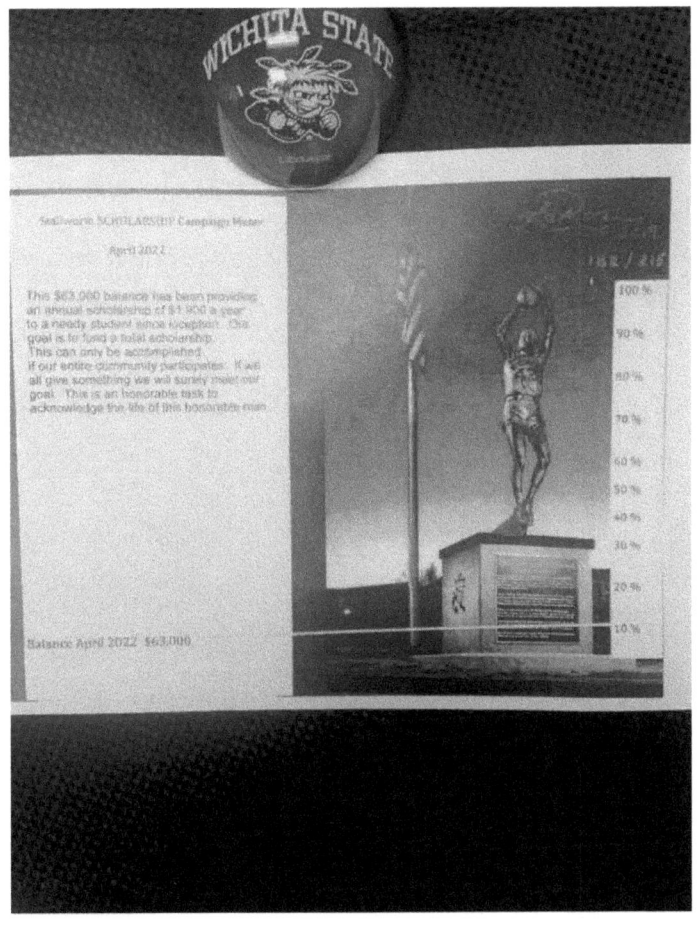

**"By the inch, it's a cinch; by the yard, it is hard"**

The population of Wichita, Kansas, is 400,564

5% or 20,028 are super loyal Shocker fans

If half of the super Shocks fans gave $60 each

**Goal Met!**

# Shocker All-Americans

## The tradition continues!

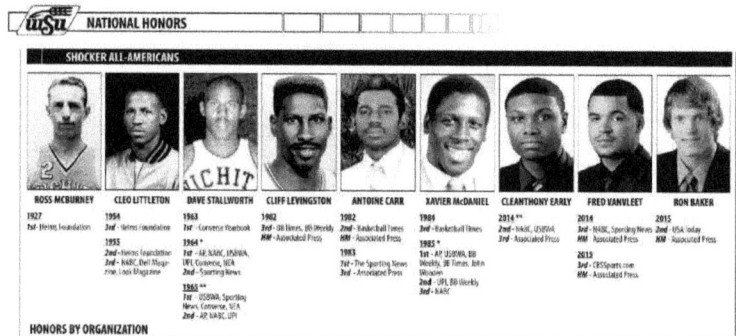

Bob Powers, Darrien Davis, first recicpient Nick Jimenez, donor

First scholarship recipient in front of Charles Koch Arena

Dave Dahl

**Husband, father, judge, attorney, "Voice of the Shockers"**

1969-70 Shocker basketball team

Blondie far left

One final note, which Bob Powers has been looking to communicate about for years. "WALK-ONS". I know three personally. Manny Zafiros on my 64-65 team. Gary Austerman 66-67 Shocker team and Dave Dahl 69-70 Shocker team. It is obvious all of them have a personal drive to succeed which goes far beyond the average human being. Each has become hugely successful in his business and personal life. What amazes me to this day is what type of character it takes for an 18-year-old to go to work three hours every day, take verbal and physical insults without pay, and have little prospect of ever playing in a real game. I will never understand how they do it. Early on, I just didn't pay attention. My respect for these individuals has grown exponentially, not just these three but all walk-ons. They are totally committed athletes. Many on scholarship would do well to follow their example.

# About the Authors

**Robert Powers**

Robert Michael Powers was born February 19, 1945, to Master Sergeant Robert John and Catherine Marsden Powers on Camp Lejeune, North Carolina. He is the oldest of seven children, with three brothers and three sisters. He earned his Bachelor of Science in Education from Wichita State University and his Master of Science in Psychology from Emporia State University.

Brothers and sisters, all college graduates:

Steven, born 1946: VMI, full basketball scholarship, graduated 1968

John, born 1949: George Washington U, full basketball scholarship, graduated 1971

Paul, born 1950: California State University of Pennsylvania, graduated 1973

Cathy, born 1955: Indiana University of Pennsylvania, graduated 1975

Debbie, born 1958: Indiana University of Pennsylvania, graduated 1980

Mary, born 1960: Trenton State University, graduated 1983

Robert Powers and his wife Joann have been blessed with eight children and 24 grandchildren, first great-grandchild. The picture below of Ben Powers, one of Bob's grandchildren, an All-American tackle at the University of Oklahoma, and at this writing, playing in his 4$^{th}$ year in the NFL, was taken at Ben's wedding (to Jayce) In April 2021. Given the size of the Powers' family, it is the best and most recent photo of all its members.

The Bob & JoAnn Powers family

April 2021

Bob and Joann Powers

## Robert Litan

Robert Litan was born to David and Shirley Litan in Wichita, Kansas on May 16, 1950. He and his brother, the late Michael Litan, were raised in McPherson, Kansas, until 1955, when the family moved to Wichita.

Bob attended Wichita Southeast High School. He later earned his B.S. in Economics at the Wharton School of Finance at the University of Pennsylvania in Philadelphia, his J.D. from Yale Law School, and his M. Phil. And Ph.D. degrees in Economics from Yale University.

Bob has had a long career as a lawyer (specializing primarily in antitrust law) and economist in the private, public and non-profit sectors. Among his many positions, Bob has served on the president's Council of Economic Advisers staff, as the principal deputy assistant attorney general in the Antitrust Division of the Department of Justice, and as associate director of the Office of Management and Budget. He also was vice president and director of research for nearly a decade at the Kauffman Foundation in Kansas City and directed research for Bloomberg Government in Washington, D.C.

Bob is the author or co-author of 29 books (counting this one) and over 300 articles in journals, magazines, newspapers, and various online outlets. At this writing, he is a Shareholder of Berger Montague, a law firm based in Philadelphia, and a non-resident senior fellow in the Economic Studies program at the Brookings Institution, a program he once directed as vice president and where he was a full-time senior fellow for over 20 years.

Bob is married to his high school sweetheart (and long-time hoops fan) Margaret and has two children, Ari and Alisa, and at this writing, four grandchildren (one of many ways in which he will never catch up to his co-author).

All his life, this smile was Dave's greatest asset.

During the last months of Dave's life, which I did not know to be his final months, I would ask him, "How do you cope with all your health issues?"

Without hesitation, he would say, "Bob, just keep doin' what you're doin'."

I never understood what he meant. I never got the chance to ask him.

David Stallworth

# 42

Born December 20, 1941

Died March 15th, 2017

College Career Statistics

79 Games

24.3 points, 10.5 rebounds, 5.9 assists per game

Much more than his stats:

Soft-spoken, gentle, always a kind word. A smile like no other. It is hard to believe that a man with a killer instinct, a streak of brutality, peasant toughness, and a strong finisher could be such a gentle human being. Only a good and gracious God could have created this gentle spirit.

God bless you, David Stallworth.

# A Final Note

This book would not be complete without honoring our seven favorite sports aficionados.

### SUELLENTROP& LUTZ

No, this is not the name of a law firm. It is, however, the name of two of the most loyal Shocker sportswriters in our community over the last 50 years.

Lutz retired but is very active with his LEAGUE 42. A sports baseball organization offering a summer of fun and training. The only requirement to join is that you must have total commitment.

Paul Suellentrop is a writer for STRATEGIC COMMUNICATIONS at Wichita State University. He and his bride, C Y, have committed their lives over the next several years to parenting an exchange student from Uganda.

Mike Kennedy has over 40 years of play-by-play broadcasting for Wichita State. My favorite memory of Mike (circa 1960s-70s) is as the skinny red-headed kid running around over at 17$^{th}$ street working for KMUW

Dave Dahl is an attorney, commentator, judge, former Shocker basketball player, and color commentator for the Shocker basketball team/

Michael Zarich Video Productions
Craig Hacker Photography
Gerald McCoy Photography

www.ingramcontent.com/pod-product-compliance
Lightning Source LLC
Chambersburg PA
CBHW041140110526
44590CB00027B/4080